WHISPER
of Wealth

AF104086

Yash Vardhan Poddar

BLUEROSE PUBLISHERS
U.K.

Copyright © Yash Vardhan Poddar 2025

All rights reserved by author. No part of this publication may be reproduced, stored in a retrieval system or transmitted in any form or by any means, electronic, mechanical, photocopying, recording or otherwise, without the prior permission of the author. Although every precaution has been taken to verify the accuracy of the information contained herein, the publisher assumes no responsibility for any errors or omissions. No liability is assumed for damages that may result from the use of information contained within.

BlueRose Publishers takes no responsibility for any damages, losses, or liabilities that may arise from the use or misuse of the information, products, or services provided in this publication.

For permissions requests or inquiries regarding this publication, please contact:

BLUEROSE PUBLISHERS
www.BlueRoseONE.com
info@bluerosepublishers.com
+4407342408967

ISBN: 978-93-7139-169-6

Cover design: Daksh
Typesetting: Tanya Raj Upadhyay

First Edition: June 2025

Acknowledgement

"I would like to extend my deepest gratitude to my family and loved ones who have supported me throughout this journey.

Firstly, to my beloved grandfather, Mr. B.N. Poddar, whose wisdom, blessings, and legacy have been a constant source of inspiration.

To my parents, Mr. Shiv Kumar Poddar and Mrs. Deepa Poddar, your unwavering encouragement, guidance, and belief in me have been invaluable.

To my siblings, Tanushree and Harsh Vardhan, your contributions, feedback, and love have enriched my work in countless ways.

I am also grateful to my friends who have been a source of strength, motivation, and joy throughout this journey.

Furthermore, I would like to acknowledge the nurturing environment provided by Saint Joseph School, where I developed my passion for learning and growth.

Thank you all for your instrumental roles in bringing this book to life."

✍ Author's Note

I didn't write this story to showcase perfect endings. I wrote it for those who begin despite everything stacked against them.

Whisper of Wealth is for dreamers who put survival first, for parents who quietly believe, and for children whose brilliance blooms in silence. Raghav is fictional — but his journey is real for many.

Carry this story with you. Into schools. Into homes. Into boardrooms. Because stories like his deserve to be heard — and remembered.

— *The Author*

💌 Reader's Note

Dear Reader,

You might find yourself in Raghav's village or his future. This book asks only one thing: be present.

Read slowly. Let the silences speak. This isn't a hero's tale — it's a quiet revolution. One where the overlooked begin to rewrite the rules.

Thank you for listening.

With all my gratitude,
The Storyteller

📖 Introduction

Somewhere in India, a boy is building something that won't make it to a PowerPoint slide. He's doing it between shifts, between silence and survival, with no promise of success.

Whisper of Wealth follows Raghav — a village boy turned innovator — not through miracles, but moments. This isn't a story of sudden triumph. It's a story of belief — stubborn, quiet, and real.

Why did I write it?

Because I was tired of stories that start at success. I wanted to write a story that starts with silence — and watches it bloom.

🎭 Cast of Characters

- **Raghav Mishra** – Village boy, self-taught coder, chasing dreams through adversity.

- **Anika** – Supportive friend in Mumbai, bright, kind, and encouraging spirit.

- **Raghav's Father** – Stern but caring, silently sacrifices for Raghav's future.

- **Raghav's Mother** – Gentle strength, quietly believes in Raghav's hidden potential.

- **Raghav's Grandfather** – Symbol of courage, remembered through his silver trishul pendant.

- **Mr. Kapoor** – Sharp investor, questions practicality of Raghav's educational app.

- **Guest Speaker** – Inspiring entrepreneur, motivates Raghav during moment of doubt.

- **Study Group Members** – Friends who help Raghav learn, grow, and belong.

- **Madhopur Villagers** – Initially doubtful, later proud of Raghav's achievements.

- **Innovation Center Faculty** – Mentors and critics shaping students' journeys and innovations.

Preface

It all began with a question I couldn't shake: *What if the next great innovator lives in a village we've never mapped – dreaming by candlelight, coding in silence?*

That question stayed with me. Into classrooms full of memorized answers, into homes where ambition felt like luxury, into boardrooms where real voices rarely enter.

Whisper of Wealth is my response.

Though Raghav is fictional, his struggles are lived by thousands. Every error he debugged, every doubt he fought — I've seen them all.

This isn't a tale of glory. It's a story of grit. For those told to be "realistic." For those tired of being statistics.

Because the greatest wealth we can ever whisper into the world is belief.

Table of Contents

Chapter 1: The Silent Coder 3

Chapter 2: The Letter That Changed Everything 9

Chapter 3: The City of Gods and Ghosts 16

Chapter 4: The First Fall and the Rising Flame 23

Chapter 5: A Glimmer Amidst the Storm 29

Chapter 6: The Weight of Dreams 35

Chapter 7: Crossroads of Commitment 40

Chapter 8: The Price of Progress 45

Chapter 9: Breaking Barriers 56

Chapter 10: Voices on the Threshold 61

Chapter 11: Turning Tides 65

Chapter 12: Seeds of Doubt 70

Chapter 13: The Storm Beneath Still Waters 82

Chapter 14: The Firefly Paradox 87

Chapter 15: Shadows in the Light 92

Chapter 16: The Crossroads of Conviction 97

Chapter 17: Tectonic Shifts 102

Chapter 18: The Echoes of Yesterday 108

Chapter 19: Winds of Change 113

Chapter 20: The Fire Beneath the Ashes 117

Chapter 21: The Light We Carry 123

Chapter 22: The Turning Point 128

Chapter 23: Fractures and Fault Lines 135

Chapter 24: Whispers from Home 142

Chapter 25: The Pivot 149

Chapter 26: The Spark of Scale 157

Chapter 27: Storms and Sacrifice 165

Chapter 28: The Phoenix Pact 173

Chapter 29: Ghosts of Greatness 180

Chapter 30: The Echo Effect 187

Chapter 31: The Whisper of Wealth 194

Final Conclusion of The Book 200

"Wealth is not just about riches,
but about the whispers of wisdom that guide us
to true prosperity and a life of purpose."

Chapter 1:
The Silent Coder

The air in Madhopur was thick with dust and history.

It was a place where mornings arrived not with the chirping of birds, but with the creaking of iron hand pumps and the muffled bleating of goats. Small homes huddled under fading blue skies, the bricks so worn they seemed like old men resting after a long life. It was the kind of village that maps forgot, that politicians remembered only during election seasons, and where dreams, if born, often died unnoticed.

But somewhere on the eastern edge of this village, in a house that smelled faintly of burnt oil and turmeric, a boy sat cross-legged on a faded charpai, his eyes fixed on a flickering laptop screen that had no brand name.

The machine was a relic, salvaged from a scrap dealer in Patna, its fan perpetually whirring like it was gasping for breath. But Raghav Mishra didn't care. For him, that ancient device was a window into a universe where limitations dissolved. Its cracked keys were like piano notes to a silent symphony he had been composing for years—one where code replaced circumstance, and logic offered a kind of freedom life had never promised.

He moved like a whisper. No one in the house noticed him much, not because they didn't love him, but because love here meant survival, not celebration. His father, a stoic man with hands that looked like they'd been carved from dry bark, was already at the grain mill. His mother stirred a pot of watery dal in the kitchen, singing a folk song to herself that sounded like a prayer wrapped in melody.

"Raghav," she called, not even looking up. "Go bring the dry clothes from the roof."

He didn't answer immediately. His fingers paused mid-code, eyes narrowing at a red error line on the screen.

"Bas do minute, Ma," he finally said, his tone quiet, respectful, distracted.

She didn't press. She never did. For all the mystery surrounding her son's obsession with that dying laptop, she had come to accept it the way villagers accept the monsoon—unpredictable, disruptive, but somehow necessary.

The code was simple today. Just a small Python script to clean up satellite data he'd downloaded illegally over a 2G network. He was trying to predict rainfall patterns by analyzing historical moisture data. It was for no one. There was no audience, no deadline, and certainly no teacher. Only him, and his stubborn desire to make sense of a world that offered none.

He had taught himself everything—how to bypass paywalls, how to install Ubuntu from a pen drive found in the trash, and how to write code that didn't crash after the first run. It wasn't brilliance. It was hunger, the kind that gnaws not at your stomach, but at your soul.

The village kids called him "chhupa scientist"—the hidden scientist. Not out of awe, but mockery. His silence unnerved them, his lack of social grace confused them. At seventeen, Raghav barely spoke unless spoken to. But when he did, his words had weight—not because they were profound, but because they were rare.

He wasn't quiet because he had nothing to say.

He was quiet because no one asked him the right questions.

After retrieving the sun-dried clothes, Raghav climbed down the ladder and folded them with care. A small bird was trapped under the tin shade, fluttering helplessly. He cupped it gently in his hands, opened the window, and let it fly.

He watched it disappear into the orange-gray sky with a longing he didn't understand.

That evening, his father returned early, a grim look on his face and grease on his kurta.

"Mill ka motor jal gaya," he muttered.

The motor had burned again.

Raghav's eyes flicked to the iron box of expenses they kept on the top shelf. Empty, most likely. The repairs would cost more than they could afford. Again.

His father didn't look at him as he washed his hands under the pump, the water sputtering like it too was tired of flowing. But there was a quiet heaviness in the air, a wordless understanding between them. Raghav knew it wasn't his job to fix the mill. But it had been years since his father stopped saying that out loud.

Over dinner, they sat on the floor, eating rice and salt. There was no meat, not even lentils. Just silence and the sound of spoons scraping steel plates.

"Computer chal raha hai?" his father asked suddenly.

Raghav nodded.

"Achha hai," the man said, staring into the distance. "Kaam aayega kabhi."

That was all. No questions about what he was building. No curiosity. Just faith—muted and buried under fatigue.

Later that night, after the kerosene lamp flickered out and the house fell into sleep, Raghav stayed awake.

His screen lit his face in blue as he scanned a webpage that had just loaded after twelve minutes. A scholarship form. An all-India innovation program in Mumbai. Full sponsorship. Open to students from rural areas with proof of independent innovation.

They wanted a short essay, a project brief, and a video.

Raghav didn't have fancy credentials. He didn't have polished grammar. He didn't even have a functioning webcam.

But he had something else.

He had nothing left to lose

He spent the next three nights writing and rewriting his essay in a tattered notebook, translating his thoughts from Hindi to English with the help of Google Translate and sheer will. He explained how his crude AI model could help farmers predict rainfall and avoid crop loss. He recorded a video on a neighbor's smartphone, speaking slowly, nervously, trying not to stutter. He didn't smile once. It wasn't intentional. It was just that the idea of "impressing" someone was alien to him.

He uploaded the files, clicked submit, and whispered a silent prayer—not to God, but to the logic that lived inside machines. They were cold, yes, but they were fair.

A week passed. Then two. Life moved on. The mill got fixed with borrowed money. The laptop overheated one night and shut down. Raghav thought maybe that was a sign to stop.

But on the fifteenth day, something arrived.

A letter.

Official. Sealed. Real.

He opened it with trembling fingers as his mother looked on. His father stood still, like a tree in shock.

Raghav had been selected.

Fully funded. Housing included. Travel reimbursed.

Destination: Mumbai.

He read the letter three times, each time slower than before. His father's face cracked open into something that looked like pride but was laced with fear. His mother cried, her tears wetting the edges of the paper.

That night, Raghav didn't code. He didn't read. He didn't sleep.

He just lay on the charpai, staring at the sky through the open window. The stars looked closer somehow. Not because he had reached them, but because—for the first time—he believed they might actually be real.

And reachable.

Chapter 2:
The Letter That Changed Everything

The village was never quiet, not truly. Even in the early hours before the sun breached the thatched rooftops, there were murmurs—the sound of roosters, the creak of wooden carts, distant temple bells battling with the static from old radios.

But that morning, Madhopur stood still.

It was the first time Raghav Mishra woke up to silence.

The letter lay on the tin trunk at the foot of his bed, still in its envelope, as if it needed time to adjust to the air of this place. It bore an official emblem and a return address from somewhere in Bandra West, Mumbai. The paper was thick, the print sharp. It didn't belong here—not on bedsheets patched with scraps, not beside slippers mended with wire.

Raghav hadn't slept. His mind had run in loops all night, retracing the moment he read the first line: *"We are pleased to inform you..."*

He knew English well enough now to understand what those words meant. But what he didn't understand—

what his brain refused to accept—was that someone in the outside world had actually seen him.

Him. Raghav. From the place where Google Maps blurred out details and couriers often gave up.

He stepped outside barefoot. The sky was smeared with charcoal gray, the sun dragging itself up like it, too, wasn't sure it wanted to rise. A dog barked somewhere near the temple. Two kids ran past him chasing a deflated football. Life, it seemed, hadn't read the letter.

Inside the kitchen, his mother stood beside the stove, her hands still stained with yesterday's turmeric. She didn't speak. She simply handed him a plate—two dry rotis and a smear of pickle—and placed a glass of goat's milk next to it.

Her silence was thicker than usual.

"You read it again?" she asked, wiping her hands on her saree.

Raghav nodded.

"And?"

"It's real," he said softly, still unsure if speaking about it might make it vanish.

She sat down across from him, resting her elbows on her knees, her eyes watching him like he was something fragile she'd never fully understood.

"Your father thinks it's risky," she said, finally. "He says Mumbai is a place where boys get lost. Where people forget where they came from."

Raghav didn't respond. Not because he agreed or disagreed, but because he knew she wasn't asking for his opinion—she was voicing her own fear through his father's voice.

He had always known this day might come. That one small window might open and show him the sky. What he hadn't prepared for was the feeling of guilt rising with his joy. He couldn't unsee the cracks in the walls, the faded school certificates pinned above his bed, or the way his father came home each night with one more layer of fatigue etched into his spine.

"Did I ask for too much?" he wondered. "Is ambition a kind of betrayal?"

By afternoon, the news had spread.

Not through social media or newspapers—those didn't travel fast in Madhopur—but through mouths.

By the time he walked to the tea stall near the post office, people were already pointing at him like he was a visiting dignitary. Some clapped him on the back, others asked for his photograph with the letter. Someone even joked, "Don't forget us when you become Bill Gates!"

He smiled politely, but inside, he was shrinking.

The attention felt sharp, unnatural. It wasn't the kind of pride that lifted him—it was the kind that placed him on a pedestal he hadn't asked for. And all pedestals were just platforms waiting to collapse.

His father didn't speak until dinner.

They sat facing each other across a steel plate of rice and boiled potatoes. The room was lit by a lone CFL bulb, flickering with every gust of wind that slipped through the wooden window frame.

"You will go?" his father asked, finally.

"I want to," Raghav said, trying to meet his eyes.

His father chewed slowly, as if buying time.

"This... this computer work of yours. Will it bring food to our table?"

Raghav swallowed. "Not today. Maybe not tomorrow. But one day—yes."

There was no arrogance in his tone. Just belief, quiet and resolute.

His father leaned back, staring at the ceiling, as if looking for wisdom among the cobwebs. Then, without warning, he stood, walked to the corner shelf, and pulled out a small tin box.

Inside was a stack of old notes, bundled with fading rubber bands. A savings fund scraped together over years—for emergencies, for family, for repairs that never came cheap.

He placed it on the table. "Take what you need."

Raghav froze.

"I'll get a little extra from the grain traders," his father continued, almost offhandedly. "You'll need shoes. Decent ones. Don't go looking like you came from nowhere."

Raghav blinked quickly. The box wasn't just money. It was permission.

The next morning, he packed.

There wasn't much. Two shirts, one pair of jeans, a book of handwritten code snippets, and the laptop wrapped in old cloth like a newborn. His mother had stitched a cloth bag for his charger and pens. She placed it in his backpack without a word, her lips pressed tight.

Just before he left, she placed a tiny silver trishul pendant in his palm.

"Keep this in your wallet," she said. "It's not magic. But it belonged to your grandfather. He never let anyone cheat him."

At the railway station, the platform was a swarm of lives colliding—vendors yelling, engines groaning, families crying at departures. Raghav had never seen this many people in one place before. The chaos overwhelmed him. So many stories, and he was just one of them.

His ticket was folded in his back pocket. Sleeper class. Upper berth.

When the train pulled in, he hugged his father stiffly. The man held him a little longer than expected.

"Learn everything," he said. "But forget nothing."

Then came his mother's arms—tight, trembling. She didn't speak. She pressed her forehead to his chest for a second, as if trying to record his heartbeat before it left.

And then he boarded.

As the train pulled away, Raghav watched the village shrink, the fields blurring into green smears, the station vanishing behind a curve.

He didn't know what lay ahead. He had never been to a city where people wore suits or attended pitch meetings. He had never tasted sushi or used an elevator. He didn't know how to talk to investors, or that they would one day try to buy what he hadn't even built yet.

All he knew was that he was leaving behind everything familiar—not to escape it, but to earn the right to return.

He opened his bag and pulled out the letter one last time.

The words were still there. Real. Heavy. Unbelievable.

You have been selected...

Somewhere deep inside, Raghav whispered back:

"So be it."

Chapter 3:
The City of Gods and Ghosts

The train screeched to a halt at Mumbai Central Station, and for a moment, Raghav Mishra simply sat still, gripping the worn leather strap of his bag as if it was the only anchor holding him steady. The air was thick with a thousand scents: pungent spices, the sour tang of garbage, the sharp bite of exhaust fumes, and the faint salty breeze drifting in from the Arabian Sea. All of it collided in his nostrils, flooding his senses in a way he had never experienced before.

The station was a swirling hive of humanity. People pushed past one another with determined urgency — mothers clutching children close, hawkers shouting their wares in rapid-fire Marathi and Hindi, porters hefting heavy loads onto carts with practiced ease. The screeching of train wheels, the distant clang of metal, and the ceaseless chatter blended into a symphony of chaos. Raghav felt as if he had stepped into another world, one where time moved at a furious pace and the usual rules no longer applied.

He swallowed hard. This was Mumbai — the City of Dreams, the City of Gods and Ghosts. A place where destinies were made and shattered beneath the relentless glare of ambition and survival.

His footsteps echoed on the cracked concrete of the station platform as he joined the tide of people moving toward the city's heart. The sky above was a dull gray, heavy with the promise of rain, and the looming skyscrapers carved jagged silhouettes against the horizon. It was impossible not to feel dwarfed by the towering buildings, their glass facades reflecting the restless city below. Raghav's heart beat unevenly, caught between awe and fear.

He adjusted the strap on his bag and stepped into the crush of humanity, moving carefully not to lose his footing. The streets outside the station were alive with vibrant colors — bright yellow taxis honked impatiently, street vendors hawked fragrant snacks, and the chatter of multiple languages intertwined like a tapestry.

Raghav's gaze drifted to a small roadside temple nestled between a dilapidated building and a modern glass office tower. A group of elderly men sat around a chessboard under the shade of a neem tree, their eyes sharp despite the heat. The temple's bells tinkled softly, mixing with the distant sound of a devotional song playing from a nearby shop's speakers.

This city was a living contradiction — ancient and modern, sacred and profane — and Raghav was both a stranger and a seeker within it.

The hostel where Raghav was to stay was hidden down a narrow alleyway that reeked of damp earth and garbage. As he pushed open the creaking door, the scent of stale air and old wood filled his lungs. The room itself was small, barely large enough to hold a single bed, a rickety table, and a chair with one broken leg. The walls were stained, and a single ceiling fan rotated lazily above, doing little to ease the heavy humidity.

Yet, to Raghav, this modest space was a sanctuary — the threshold to a life he had dared to dream about. He unpacked his few belongings carefully: a couple of worn shirts, a notebook filled with scribbled ideas, the old silver trishul his mother had pressed into his palm before he left.

He touched the pendant reverently, feeling the cold metal against his skin, a talisman to ward off fear and doubt.

That evening, the city unveiled itself further. Stepping out, Raghav wandered along the crowded streets lined with shops bursting with color and life. Women in vibrant saris bustled about, their bangles jingling; children darted between the legs of rickshaws and bicycles; street cooks flipped vadas and dosas with practiced flicks of their wrists, filling the air with the aroma of frying spices.

He bought a cup of steaming chai from a vendor whose weathered face smiled kindly at him. The warmth seeped into his fingers, a small comfort against the cold edge of homesickness that gnawed at his heart.

As he sipped, Raghav watched a group of young men and women laughing loudly outside a nearby café. Their faces shone with the bright confidence of those who belonged here. He yearned to be one of them, to shed the shyness and uncertainty that clung to him like a shadow.

The following morning dawned with a leaden sky and a damp chill in the air. Raghav arrived at the sprawling campus of the tech innovation institute, a cluster of glass buildings gleaming under the faint sunlight. The manicured lawns and neatly paved paths contrasted starkly with the chaos of the city beyond the gates.

Inside the lecture hall, he found himself overwhelmed by the sheer scale of ambition. Students whispered excitedly about machine learning algorithms, venture capital, and pitch competitions. The jargon felt like a foreign language, their confidence only highlighting his own sense of inadequacy.

He sat quietly in the back, absorbing every word, afraid to speak for fear of stumbling over his accent or revealing his gaps in knowledge.

During lunch, Raghav found himself sitting alone on a bench under a tall banyan tree. His eyes traced the intricate patterns of the leaves filtering the sunlight in fractured shadows. The distant buzz of conversations and the scent of freshly cooked food mingled with the hum of passing traffic.

A voice interrupted his solitude.

"Hey, you're new here, right?"

He looked up to see a girl with lively eyes and an easy smile. She was holding a tiffin box and wore a casual hoodie emblazoned with the institute's logo.

"I'm Anika," she said, sliding down beside him. "I noticed you at orientation. Don't worry, we've all been the new kid at some point."

Raghav smiled shyly, the weight of loneliness lifting just a fraction.

"Would you like to join us for some study sessions? It's easier when you have friends."

Over the next few weeks, Raghav began to unravel the tangled threads of his new life. Mornings were spent in rigorous classes that stretched his understanding of coding and data structures. Afternoons found him huddled in the library, poring over textbooks, occasionally glancing at his phone to catch messages from his parents.

Evenings became moments of quiet reflection or bursts of nervous laughter with Anika and her friends. They shared stories of distant homes, of struggles and triumphs, of dreams tethered by reality.

Mumbai itself became a character in his story — its rains soaking the streets and turning alleys into shimmering rivers, its festivals lighting up the night sky, its relentless energy both exhausting and exhilarating.

But with every step forward came the pangs of doubt. Raghav grappled with his own limitations, the weight of expectations pressing down on him. The polished presentations of his classmates made him feel raw and unprepared. The mentors' questions sometimes felt like traps designed to expose his inexperience.

One evening, after a particularly harsh critique, he wandered aimlessly until he found himself at a small temple tucked between two glass towers. The smell of sandalwood incense filled the air, and the soft murmur of prayers offered a refuge.

Lighting a candle, he clutched the silver trishul beneath his shirt and whispered a plea for strength — a promise to himself that he would endure, that he would grow beyond the boy who had once been too afraid to dream.

Slowly, the city began to reveal its hidden kindnesses. Anika introduced him to more friends, people who came from places like him, who understood the quiet battles behind every smile. Together, they shared late-night coding sessions fueled by instant noodles and stubborn hope.

Raghav found himself laughing again, daring to envision a future that was no longer just a distant fantasy but a tangible possibility.

On a rainy monsoon evening, standing on the rooftop of their hostel, Raghav looked out over the city sprawled beneath him. The lights twinkled like a thousand fireflies, and the rain cast a shimmering veil over the streets.

Here, amidst the gods and ghosts of Mumbai, Raghav Mishra felt something stirring deep inside — a fierce determination to rise, to belong, to turn his potential into reality.

No matter the obstacles, this was his city now. And he was ready to fight for his place within it.

Chapter 4:
The First Fall and the Rising Flame

The first rays of sunlight seeped hesitantly through the narrow, dust-speckled windowpanes of the innovation center. The old building, with its peeling paint and creaky ceiling fans, seemed like a world away from the sprawling metropolis outside. Yet within these walls, dreams were born, crushed, and reborn every day. Rows of desks stretched in neat lines, cluttered with the paraphernalia of young creators — laptops with stickers peeling at the edges, notebooks filled with diagrams and scrawled ideas, and half-empty cups of chai stained with lipstick marks.

Raghav sat at his usual corner desk, a small fortress of scattered papers and tangled wires surrounding him. His fingers hovered uncertainly over the keyboard, but no code came. His eyes darted to the screen, where red error messages blinked accusingly, refusing to yield to his persistent attempts. He had been at it for weeks, pouring every waking moment into perfecting his project — an app designed to help rural students access personalized education in their native languages. This was more than a project; it was a promise to his village, to his family, to himself.

But today, the code was a stubborn beast. Every fix he tried only unearthed new problems. Frustration gnawed at him, sharp and relentless. Doubt whispered insidiously at the edges of his resolve. Maybe he wasn't cut out for this after all.

His phone buzzed on the desk. He glanced down — a message from his mother: *"Beta, we are praying for you. Don't give up."* The words were soft but heavy, carrying the weight of sacrifice. His family had mortgaged their small farm to send him here, to Mumbai, to a future they could only dream of. Failure was not just personal; it was a betrayal of their hopes.

He looked up as the room grew noisier. Groups of students gathered near the presentation boards, rehearsing pitches with nervous energy. The walls echoed with debates over ideas, the clatter of keyboards, and bursts of laughter. Success was celebrated here, failure hushed or ignored.

When it was Raghav's turn to present, his heart pounded fiercely in his chest. Standing before a small group of visiting investors and faculty, his voice trembled as he began. The words felt heavy, clumsy on his tongue. He stumbled over technical jargon, flinched at pointed questions about scalability and revenue models, and struggled to keep eye contact. The investors listened politely, their expressions unreadable, but the polite nods felt cold, distant.

When he finished, a silence stretched uncomfortably before a few faint claps echoed from the back. Raghav's cheeks burned. He sat back down, shoulders slumped. Nearby, he overheard whispers — "Too inexperienced," "Can't communicate well," "Idea needs more polish." Each word pricked him like thorns.

The day's failure pressed heavily on his spirit. As evening settled, the sky darkened with thick monsoon clouds, and a soft rain began to fall, turning the dusty streets slick and shimmering. Raghav walked aimlessly through the crowded lanes near his hostel, the neon signs reflecting in puddles, the air thick with the mingled scents of wet earth, spices, and exhaust fumes.

Seeking refuge from the damp chill, he slipped into a small roadside café tucked between a bookstore and a tailor's shop. The place was warm, filled with the comforting murmur of patrons and the sharp hiss of chai being poured from steaming kettles. He ordered a cup, the fragrant steam wrapping around him like a gentle hug.

An elderly man sitting alone at the next table glanced over and smiled kindly. "First time here?" he asked, his voice low but inviting.

Raghav nodded shyly.

"Don't let the city's noise drown your dreams," the man said. "Every one of us has fallen hard at some point. The question is — will you rise?"

Raghav looked into the man's eyes, seeing a reflection of his own fears and hopes. The words sank deep, planting a fragile seed of courage.

That night, the monsoon rains hammered relentlessly against the hostel's corrugated iron roof. Raghav lay awake, the distant thunder rolling like the storm within his heart. He stared at the cracked ceiling, tracing imaginary constellations in the peeling paint, his mind drifting to his village—fields of golden wheat swaying under the sun, the ancient banyan tree beneath which elders had told stories, and his mother's lullabies that had once wrapped him in warmth.

Mumbai was different—harsh, relentless, and unforgiving. The city's endless pulse was both exhilarating and alienating. Could a boy from a small village survive here? Could he thrive?

His fingers brushed the silver trishul resting on the bedside table, the metal cool and solid beneath his palm. He whispered a prayer, asking for strength, for clarity, for the grit to keep fighting.

The next morning, a pale mist hung over the city. Vendors set up their stalls along the narrow lanes, filling the air with the aroma of freshly fried samosas and sweet jalebis. Raghav wrapped his thin jacket tighter and stepped out, the familiar chaos of Mumbai greeting him like an old, unpredictable friend.

His phone buzzed with a message from his father: *"Patience and perseverance turn seeds into trees. Keep going, son."*

A small smile touched his lips. Those simple words, spoken so many times back home, now felt like a lifeline.

Inside the lecture hall, an unusual buzz filled the air. A guest speaker — a successful entrepreneur who had risen from humble beginnings — was scheduled to share his journey. The room filled quickly with eager students, faces bright with anticipation.

Raghav took a seat near the back, his curiosity tempered by the cautious hope blossoming inside him.

The speaker, a man with a commanding presence and eyes full of fire, began. "I come from a small town, much like many of you. I failed repeatedly — I was rejected, mocked, told to quit. But each 'no' was a lesson, each stumble a step forward."

His voice grew stronger. "Success isn't a straight path. It's messy, full of detours and setbacks. If you can embrace failure, you'll find a strength you never knew existed."

The talk ignited something in the room, a fresh wave of energy. Students clustered in small groups, sharing ideas and encouragement. Anika found Raghav and smiled warmly. "Ready to rewrite your story?"

Together, they spent hours breaking down problems into manageable pieces, debugging lines of code, and brainstorming new solutions. Failure was no longer an endpoint but a signpost on the road ahead.

Months passed. Mumbai's relentless rhythm became both a challenge and a teacher. Raghav's skills sharpened, and though setbacks still came, they no longer crushed him. Presentations faltered, code crashed — but every fall was softer, cushioned by friendships and steady progress.

One evening, atop the hostel's rooftop, the city sprawled beneath a sky heavy with monsoon clouds. Lights flickered like distant stars, rain pattering softly on the tarpaulin roof. Raghav and Anika sat side by side, wrapped in blankets.

"I'm starting to believe," he said quietly, eyes fixed on the horizon.

Anika smiled. "That belief is the first step toward changing your story."

The city breathed around them — a living mosaic of dreams and struggles, failures and triumphs. For Raghav, every challenge was a chapter in his unfolding story — one of resilience, courage, and the relentless pursuit of potential.

Chapter 5:
A Glimmer Amidst the Storm

The monsoon had transformed Mumbai into a city of shimmering reflections and endless rain. Streets became rivers, and the relentless downpour blurred the harsh edges of the sprawling metropolis. From the windows of the innovation center—a modest building nestled amid towering glass giants—water trickled down in tiny rivulets, tracing unpredictable patterns across the glass like veins of the city itself.

Inside, the atmosphere was different. The room hummed with low murmurs, punctuated by the rhythmic tapping of keys, the occasional sigh, and the faint murmur of encouragement exchanged between teammates. The smell of damp clothes mixed with the lingering aroma of chai steeping in thermos flasks.

Raghav sat at his corner desk, fingers poised hesitantly above his laptop keyboard. His eyes were fixed on the screen, where a complex interface blinked back at him. This was not just any software — it was the culmination of months of painstaking work, a digital bridge meant to connect thousands of children speaking forgotten dialects to the world of education.

Anika, sitting beside him, glanced up and caught his

gaze. Her dark eyes, bright with anticipation despite the long hours and mounting setbacks, sparked a smile on his face.

"See here," Raghav said, pointing to a cluster of colorful icons. "The speech recognition algorithm. We've got it working in three dialects now — Bhojpuri, Maithili, and Tulu."

Anika leaned closer, excitement flickering in her expression. "That's huge, Raghav. It means the app can actually talk to kids in their mother tongues. They'll understand lessons better. This is the breakthrough we needed."

The weight that had settled over Raghav's chest — a mix of exhaustion, fear, and hope — lightened just a fraction. For a moment, the city's endless rain and noise faded into the background. It was just the two of them, and this fragile but promising spark of success.

But this moment had been hard-earned.

Weeks ago, the small team had stood nervously before a panel of investors in a sleek conference room. The air was sterile and cold, filled with skeptical gazes and polished suits that seemed to look right through Raghav's unpolished enthusiasm.

"Your concept is noble, but unrealistic," said Mr. Kapoor, a man with sharp eyes and a voice like gravel. "Technology for rural education has been tried before.

Infrastructure is lacking, connectivity is patchy, and users are illiterate in digital tools. How do you expect to overcome these massive barriers?"

Raghav felt the sting of doubt seeping in. His rehearsed answers seemed weak under the weight of reality.

Anika's voice cut through the tension, steady and clear. "We understand the challenges. That's why we're working with local NGOs and community leaders to adapt the app for offline use and low literacy. This isn't just a product — it's a movement to include those forgotten by mainstream education."

Mr. Kapoor studied her for a moment, then nodded slowly. "Keep refining. But be ready for the uphill battle ahead."

Those uphill battles had become their daily routine.

Late nights blurred into early mornings as the team battled bugs, code errors, and technical crashes. The hostel where Raghav stayed was cramped, the air thick with the smell of wet clothes and worn books. Instant noodles became the default dinner, broken only by occasional cups of chai brewed strong enough to keep them alert.

Still, the setbacks gnawed at him. When a critical feature failed during testing, he had felt the sharp sting of despair. But Anika's steady optimism, their shared purpose, kept pulling him forward.

One rainy evening, exhausted and soaked from the relentless monsoon, Raghav wandered through a narrow lane lined with shuttered shops and glowing street lamps. The city felt like a living, breathing entity — raw, chaotic, and unforgiving.

He stopped outside a small roadside stall selling steaming samosas and chai. The familiar aromas mingled with the fresh scent of rain-washed earth. Sitting there, wrapped in a thin shawl against the chill, he found a moment of quiet amid the chaos.

His thoughts drifted back to his childhood in Chandanpur — a village cradled between gentle hills and endless fields of wheat and millet. The memory was vivid: dusty paths where he ran barefoot, the warm laughter of children playing cricket with makeshift bats, the fading paint of the village school where the blackboard was smeared with chalk and hope.

He thought of Meera, his younger sister, struggling to learn from teachers who spoke only Hindi, a language foreign to her ears. The frustration, the confusion, and the longing in her eyes had never left him.

Anika joined him, breaking his reverie gently.

"Thinking of home?" she asked softly.

He nodded. "I want this app to reach kids like Meera. Not just in one village, but everywhere."

Her smile was small but sure. "We will make it happen.

Together."

Their journey took an unexpected turn when Mr. Kapoor returned one afternoon, this time with a different tone.

"You're making progress, but technology alone won't win this," he said. "You need to build trust. Partnerships with NGOs, local schools, community workers. People who know the terrain better than you."

That advice opened new pathways.

Raghav and Anika spent weeks traveling to rural schools, talking to teachers, children, and parents. They listened to stories of struggle and resilience. They adapted the app to work offline, simplified interfaces, and added culturally relevant content — folk stories, local songs, and games that would engage young learners

Meanwhile, the city's monsoon storms mirrored the turmoil in Raghav's heart. Funding remained tight, and the weight of expectations pressed hard. Calls home reminded him of the sacrifices his parents had made, their voices filled with hope and worry.

One late night, he sat by the window, watching raindrops race each other down the glass. His father's words echoed in his mind: *"Patience is the soil from which success grows."*

At last, the day came when the prototype worked — truly worked. Lessons flowed smoothly in local dialects, interactive exercises engaged children, and feedback from pilot users was overwhelmingly positive.

Raghav felt a swell of pride, tempered by the daunting road ahead.

As the monsoon skies began to clear, a new dawn rose for Raghav and his team — a fragile glimmer amidst the storm, a promise that their dreams might yet take flight.

Chapter 6:
The Weight of Dreams

The morning light filtered weakly through the grimy windowpanes of their cramped workspace, casting faint shadows on scattered papers and half-empty chai cups. Outside, the city stirred awake, but inside, the atmosphere was tense — thick with exhaustion and fragile hope.

Raghav sat hunched over his laptop, fingers poised but unmoving on the keyboard. His eyes were tired, rimmed red from sleepless nights and relentless worry. The prototype was working — finally — but the journey ahead loomed like a mountain too steep to climb.

Anika entered quietly, balancing two steaming cups of chai. Her face, though tired, held that spark of determination Raghav loved most.

"Still wrestling with the investor deck?" she asked softly, setting a cup beside him.

He forced a smile. "More like wrestling with doubt."

She sat down, eyes locking with his. "Talk to me."

Raghav took a slow sip, drawing warmth from the tea. "We have something real, something that can change lives. But the money... it's always the money. Investors want quick returns. They don't see the children in those remote classrooms, the ones who don't even have books."

Anika nodded knowingly. "They see numbers. Not people."

He sighed. "I don't know how to bridge that gap."

Anika's fingers found his hand. "We tell their stories."

Later that day, the pair found themselves sitting across a rough wooden table from Mrs. Kamala, a village schoolteacher whose reputation preceded her.

The classroom was modest — bare walls, a blackboard smeared with chalk dust, a few battered desks. Outside, children's laughter echoed faintly.

Kamala's eyes held a mixture of skepticism and hope. "Many come with big ideas and leave empty promises," she said. "What makes you different?"

Raghav leaned forward. "Because we listen. We don't want to replace teachers. We want to empower them."

Anika added, "Our app speaks in the languages these children know — their stories, their songs. We adapt to what they need, not what we think they need."

Kamala's expression softened. "If you truly care about these children, then I will stand with you."

Walking back through the dusty lanes, Anika whispered, "Trust is the foundation. Without it, no building stands."

Raghav's thoughts swirled — the endless paperwork, the endless calls, the weight of expectations from family and self. Yet, here was a woman willing to believe.

Days blurred into weeks of field visits, meetings, late nights filled with coding and brainstorming. They traveled to villages where electricity was a luxury, and mobile signals flickered like ghosts.

One afternoon, seated under the shade of a banyan tree, Raghav watched as a small group of children gathered around a tablet, their faces glowing with wonder as a story unfolded in their dialect.

A little girl tugged at his sleeve. "Will this help me read better?"

Raghav smiled, heart swelling. "Yes, it will. One word at a time."

Back in the city, fatigue gnawed at the team.

Anika sighed, rubbing her eyes. "We need more hands. Everyone's stretched too thin."

Priya, who had become a crucial ally, nodded in agreement. "And we need to keep spirits high. Burnout is our enemy."

They started small rituals — Friday evening meals, shared jokes, even a dance break or two.

At home, family calls brought fresh challenges.

"Raghav, you're too far from home," his mother said, voice heavy with worry. "Come back before the city swallows you."

He replied softly, "I'm fighting for our future. For children like Meera."

His father's gruff voice echoed in his mind: *"Hard work is seed. Patience is soil."*

One rainy night, power went out in their workspace. Candles flickered, shadows leapt on the walls.

Anika laughed, "Looks like the universe wants us to slow down."

Raghav smiled. "Or test our will."

In the flickering candlelight, the team found renewed strength in their shared purpose.

Months later, pilot data arrived. Engagement was growing. Children were learning, laughing, coming back for more.

At a team meeting, Priya presented the numbers. "We're reaching twice as many as last month."

Raghav's voice cracked with emotion. "This is the proof we needed."

Anika raised her cup. "To every child daring to dream."

The room echoed with quiet cheers.

Later that night, on the terrace overlooking the glittering

city, Raghav turned to Anika.

"Do you ever fear it won't last? That this spark might fade?"

She took his hand. "Every day. But then I see their faces. And I remember why we began."

He looked out at the endless lights. "Then we keep going. Together."

The weight of the dream was heavy. But so was the hope — stubborn, bright, unyielding.

Chapter 7:
Crossroads of Commitment

The rain came down in thick sheets, drumming a relentless rhythm against the rooftop of the cramped café where Raghav and Anika sought refuge. Inside, the air was thick with the smell of wet earth and brewing chai — the two scents blending into a kind of bittersweet comfort.

Raghav stared into the bottom of his cup, watching the last drops swirl like storms in a teacup. His mind was a tempest itself, a swirling mass of excitement and anxiety. EduInnovate had reached a pivotal moment — but that moment felt less like a triumph and more like standing on a cliff's edge, unsure if the next step would be a leap of faith or a fall.

Anika slid into the chair opposite him, her eyes searching his. "You've been quiet all evening," she said gently, reaching out to cover his restless hands.

He looked up and gave a tired smile. "I'm just thinking about the future. About what's at stake."

She nodded, understanding more than she could say. "It's not just about the product anymore, is it? It's about everything — the people, the promises, the trust."

Raghav took a deep breath, steadying himself. "We're meeting potential partners tonight. Priya's convinced this could be the breakthrough we need."

Anika's eyes narrowed thoughtfully. "Partners could mean more resources — but also more strings."

"Exactly," Raghav said. "They want to scale, yes, but they also want control. Control over content, decisions, the direction of the whole project."

Anika's fingers tightened around his. "So, what do we do when dreams collide with reality?"

Later that evening, the team entered a gleaming glass building downtown, worlds away from the dusty villages where their journey began. The lobby was vast and cold, echoing with footsteps and murmured greetings. The weight of formality settled over them like a second skin.

Inside the conference room, a group of suited executives awaited, their expressions polite but unreadable.

Priya stepped up first, her voice steady as she laid out the impact numbers, testimonials from teachers, and feedback from pilot programs. The room was silent except for the hum of the projector.

Then came questions: How quickly can you scale? What safeguards are in place to ensure content quality? How will you measure success?

The lead executive, Mr. Joshi, a man whose presence

seemed to fill the room, leaned forward. "Your results are promising, but scaling requires structure. We need quarterly impact reports, compliance with national education standards, and a role in content approval."

Raghav felt the sting behind the words. It was less a partnership and more a directive.

"While we appreciate the offer," he began carefully, "our mission is rooted in empowering local teachers and communities. We can't afford to compromise that."

Mr. Joshi's eyes flickered with something like respect. "We're not here to undermine you, but the foundation must ensure accountability. If this is to be a model program, it must be replicable and monitored closely."

Anika exchanged a glance with Raghav — a silent conversation about the road ahead.

The following days blurred in a haze of negotiations and sleepless nights. Their small team debated endlessly.

"We must protect our vision," Anika said fiercely. "If we surrender control, what are we left with?"

Priya responded pragmatically, "But without funding, scaling is impossible. We need to be realistic."

Raghav found himself torn between the two. His father's words echoed in his memory: *"Hard work is seed. Patience is soil. Trust the seasons."* Was this the season to stand firm or bend?

At home, the tension was no less palpable.

Raghav's mother fretted over his health and wellbeing. "You're running yourself ragged. When will you rest?"

He smiled tiredly. "Rest can wait. This work, this dream... it's bigger than me."

His father's voice, rough but wise, reminded him in an old recording: *"Son, dreams don't come cheap. You pay in sweat, sacrifice, and sometimes, heartbreak."*

One particularly bleak evening, the power failed in their office. Darkness swallowed the room except for the flicker of candles. Shadows danced on walls plastered with sketches, notes, and timelines.

Anika laughed softly, breaking the silence. "Maybe the universe wants us to slow down."

Raghav shook his head, smiling despite the gloom. "Or test our resolve."

They huddled close, telling stories of childhood dreams, their fears, and the hope that kept them moving forward.

Weeks passed, bringing tentative successes and new challenges. Technical glitches tested the app's resilience. Teachers hesitated to adopt unfamiliar technology. Feedback poured in — some hopeful, some skeptical.

During a team meeting, Priya shared a report.

"User engagement is up thirty percent, but support requests have doubled. We need better training programs."

Anika frowned. "We underestimated the learning curve."

Raghav nodded, feeling the familiar pressure settle again. "Failure isn't an option. We adapt."

At night, the terrace of their small office offered brief solace. The city's glowing skyline stretched infinitely, a reminder of both promise and loneliness.

"Do you ever doubt if this will last?" Raghav asked quietly.

Anika's eyes met his, steady and unwavering. "Every day. But then I see their faces — the children, the teachers. And I remember why we fight."

He took her hand. "Together?"

"Always."

As the monsoon clouds began to break, so too did the first true cracks in their struggle — revealing the cost of chasing a dream amid the realities of power, money, and human frailty.

Chapter 8:
The Price of Progress

The first light of dawn seeped cautiously through the tall glass windows of the EduInnovate office. Mumbai's relentless pulse was still waking up, a slow, steady thrum below the surface of a city that never truly rested. RAGHAV MISHRA sat by the window, a worn leather notebook open on his lap, his fingers tracing the faint indentations of his own scribbles made months ago.

Memories washed over him — the cramped apartment he once called home, the relentless hum of his old laptop running code that barely worked, the sleepless nights fueled by instant coffee and stubborn dreams. He closed his eyes and the past unfolded like a film.

Flashback: The Humble Beginnings

Years ago, in a small neighborhood of Pune, young Raghav had stared at a cracked screen of an aging computer. The buzzing sound was both his frustration and his fuel.

"How will I ever make this work?" he had muttered to himself. The project was ambitious: an app to help rural children learn English and math through stories and games. But the coding was buggy, the interface clunky, and the funds almost nonexistent.

His father, a modest carpenter, had entered the room with a steaming cup of chai.

"Son, progress demands patience," he said quietly, placing the cup beside Raghav. "And progress demands price."

Raghav looked up, eyes burning with determination. "I'm ready for the price, Baba."

Back in the present, the price had been steep — late nights, strained relationships, endless doubts. Yet the flicker of hope remained.

Anika Patel's soft footsteps pulled him from his thoughts.

"You look lost in memories," she smiled, setting down her own mug.

Raghav smiled back, a little wistful. "Sometimes it helps to remember why we started."

The Day Ahead

The team gathered for their morning briefing. Priya Sharma's voice cut through the quiet hum.

"We've received new feedback from the pilot schools," she announced. "Engagement is increasing, but resistance among teachers has grown."

Meera Joshi, their field coordinator, nodded. "Many

teachers feel the technology is alien — some even fear it threatens their role."

Raghav's heart sank. It was the exact problem he'd feared.

Anika leaned forward. "We need to bridge that gap. We can't let technology push them out. They have to feel empowered, not replaced."

Journey to Chandpur

That afternoon, Raghav and Anika set off to Chandpur, a small town where EduInnovate's pilot program had stalled.

The train rattled and clanked through the lush countryside, the landscape unfolding in vivid greens and golds. When they arrived, the dry dusty roads and weather-beaten buildings were a harsh contrast to Mumbai's chaos.

At the local school, Headmistress Suman awaited with a guarded smile.

"You are the ones behind this 'EduInnovate'?" she asked.

"Yes," Raghav replied respectfully. "We want to understand your experience."

Suman sighed, her eyes reflecting years of struggles. "Technology is a promise here — but also a disruption. Our teachers are wary. Some see the app as a threat to their livelihood."

Anika nodded. "We want to work *with* you. How can we make this better?"

Under the Banyan Tree

That evening, a small group of teachers gathered beneath the sprawling banyan tree, their faces illuminated by the warm glow of lanterns.

Ravi, a teacher with two decades of experience, was the first to speak.

"I've taught children all my life," he said. "But this app feels like someone else telling me how to teach."

Deepa, younger and more optimistic, added, "Maybe if the app listened to us, not just told us what to do. If we could shape it, not just use it."

Anika took careful notes, feeling the weight of their words.

"This is the price of progress," she whispered to herself. "Humility."

Return to Mumbai — Funding Crisis

Weeks later, the monsoon rains lashed the city. Inside the office, tension was thick.

Priya broke the news. "The foundation is delaying our next funding installment. They want more impact data."

Raghav stared at the screen. "We can't afford delays."

Anika said quietly, "We'll find a way. We have to."

This is just the beginning — the story will unfold with more detailed teacher profiles, community interactions, emotional highs and lows, and the relentless push forward despite setbacks.

The night in Chandpur carried a quiet hum — crickets sang softly, and the cool breeze rustled the leaves overhead. Beneath the banyan tree, the teachers' stories unfolded like threads weaving a tapestry of hopes, fears, and stubborn resolve.

Ravi, the elder teacher with silver streaks in his black hair, took a slow breath. "In my twenty years, I have seen many programs come and go. Promises made, promises broken. This new technology... it scares some of us. It feels like it will make our knowledge obsolete."

Anika listened carefully, her heart aching with the weight of his words. "I understand your fear, Ravi ji. But our goal is not to replace you but to support you. Your experience, your wisdom — that is irreplaceable."

Deepa, a younger teacher who had grown up with a smartphone in her hand, nodded in agreement. "Technology can be a tool, not a master. But only if it respects the hands that wield it."

A Night of Shared Dreams

The teachers shared stories late into the night — about their classrooms, their students, and the changes they wished to see.

Ravi talked about Raju, a boy in his class who struggled with reading. "Before the app, Raju would hide in the back, ashamed. Now, sometimes, he's the first to raise his hand."

Deepa smiled. "Technology helped Raju, but it also gave me new ways to teach him."

Anika felt a surge of hope. This was the real impact — lives touched, minds opened.

Back in Mumbai — The Pressure Mounts

Raghav paced the length of the office. The news of funding delays had rippled through the team, draining their morale.

Priya sat at her desk, her fingers poised over the keyboard. "We need a new strategy. If we can't get foundation support, maybe it's time to reach out to local NGOs or government programs."

Anika agreed. "We also need to listen more — to the teachers, to the students. Our success depends on their trust."

Raghav nodded, feeling the familiar spark of determination. "Let's plan a community outreach program. Face to face, on the ground."

The Human Cost

Late one evening, Anika sat alone in the empty office, her thoughts drifting to her sister's wedding she had missed. The sacrifices weighed heavy.

Her phone buzzed. It was a message from Priya: *"Can't make it home this weekend. Baby's sick. We're all stretched thin."*

Anika sighed. "We're paying a price," she whispered to the empty room.

A New Partnership Blossoms

Days later, a local NGO specializing in rural education expressed interest in partnering.

Their leader, Mr. Deshmukh, visited the office with a warm handshake. "We have volunteers who know these communities. We can help bridge the gap."

With this new alliance, EduInnovate planned hands-on workshops, peer-to-peer training, and culturally adapted learning materials.

Reflections on the Rooftop

One rainy evening, Raghav and Anika stood on the office rooftop, the city lights twinkling through the mist.

"Progress is never easy," Raghav said softly. "But every child who learns, every teacher who feels empowered — that makes the struggle worth it."

Anika smiled, her eyes shining. "Together, we can bear the price."

The next morning dawned bright and warm, a stark contrast to the lingering monsoon clouds that had drenched Mumbai for days. At EduInnovate's office, the energy felt different — charged with cautious optimism.

Raghav had arranged a meeting with Aarav, a teenager from one of the pilot villages, whose story had quietly become a beacon of hope for the entire team.

Aarav arrived shyly, clutching a worn-out backpack. His wide eyes darted around the bustling office before he finally settled into a chair.

"Tell us about school," Raghav began gently.

Aarav smiled, a mix of pride and embarrassment. "Before the app, I was scared to read aloud. The other kids laughed. But now... I practice with the stories every night. Sometimes, I even teach my little sister."

Anika leaned forward. "What's your favorite story?"

"The one about the brave farmer who saved his village," Aarav said, eyes brightening. "It makes me feel like I can do something important too."

Teachers, Students, and Dreams

As Aarav spoke, Priya recorded every word, capturing not just data but a glimpse of transformation.

Meera, who had accompanied Raghav to Chandpur, shared her own observations.

"Students like Aarav are the real proof that technology, combined with empathy, can create change."

Yet, challenges remained. Many children lacked access to smartphones or reliable internet. Some families worried about the time spent on screens.

Raghav listened carefully. "We need to find ways to reach those without devices — community centers, offline content, printed materials."

A Tense Meeting with Government Officials

Later that week, Raghav and Anika faced a different kind of challenge — a meeting with education ministry officials.

The room was cold and sterile. A stern-faced bureaucrat, Mr. Iyer, sat across the table.

"We appreciate your initiative," he began, "but government programs have strict guidelines. Integration with existing curricula is mandatory. And funding is limited."

Anika responded calmly, "We understand and respect the constraints. Our goal is to complement, not compete."

Raghav added, "If we work together, we can reach far more children."

After hours of negotiations, the officials agreed to pilot a joint program in select districts.

The Personal Toll

Back at the office, the pressure was mounting. Priya's baby was ill again, and Meera was juggling family responsibilities alongside fieldwork.

One evening, Anika found Raghav staring blankly at his laptop.

"Are you okay?" she asked softly.

He sighed. "Sometimes I wonder if all this is enough. If the sacrifices are worth it."

Anika placed a hand on his shoulder. "The price is high. But every child like Aarav makes it worth paying."

A Glimmer of Hope

Weeks later, EduInnovate launched community learning hubs, staffed by local volunteers trained through the NGO partnership.

At one such hub, Aarav helped younger children navigate the stories and lessons.

The village buzzed with excitement as parents and teachers gathered to watch demonstrations.

Ravi, the veteran teacher, approached Raghav.

"You've taught us something important — that progress must be patient and inclusive."

Raghav smiled, feeling the weight of years lighten just a bit.

The journey was far from over, but for the first time, the team could glimpse a future where technology and tradition walked hand in hand.

Chapter 9: Breaking Barriers

The dawn in Mumbai was a haze of golden light and distant traffic noise, as the city slowly awoke from its restless slumber. Inside the glass-paneled walls of EduInnovate's modest office, the team gathered around a large wooden table, strewn with laptops, papers, and half-empty cups of coffee. The air was thick with anticipation and urgency.

Raghav leaned forward, eyes fixed on the laptop screen that Priya was navigating. The latest data from their rural pilot schools blinked at him: attendance rates, test scores, and dropout statistics. Numbers that told a story—hope sprinkled with struggle.

"Attendance is improving," Priya said, her voice steady but concerned, "but there's a clear gender gap. Girls' attendance is still trailing boys' by nearly 20% in several districts."

Raghav rubbed his temple. "It's not just about schools or technology," he said. "We're trying to rewrite centuries of tradition and expectation."

Anika stepped into the room, her arms full of freshly printed survey results. "The community surveys confirm it. Parents worry about their daughters' safety, the loss of household help, and even social backlash."

Priya sighed. "Some families see education for girls as a luxury, not a necessity."

Raghav's gaze hardened with resolve. "If we want true change, we have to understand these fears and address them — not just with technology, but with empathy."

Journey to Navapur

That week, EduInnovate's small but determined team set out for Navapur, a village tucked away in the verdant hills of Maharashtra. The journey was long, the road winding and often rutted from the recent monsoons.

When they arrived, the village greeted them with a mix of curiosity and caution. Women in bright saris tended to the fields, children chased each other under wide banyan trees, and elders sat outside mud houses, their eyes wary but watchful.

At the village school, Headmistress Meera waited for them. She had been a steadfast ally since EduInnovate's first pilot.

"We've gathered some parents for a meeting," Meera said quietly. "They want answers."

Inside the cramped schoolhouse, wooden benches creaked under the weight of anxious mothers and fathers. The atmosphere was tense.

Raghav stood before them, heart pounding but voice

steady. "We're not here to impose change. We're here to listen and learn. What worries you about this new way of learning?"

Kamala, a middle-aged woman with weathered hands and bright eyes, rose slowly. "My daughter Anjali helps me at home — cooking, cleaning, caring for her younger siblings. Now she spends hours on a tablet. Who will help me when she is away?"

A murmur of agreement rippled through the crowd.

Anika stepped forward gently. "Kamala ji, education is not meant to take your daughter away from her family. It is meant to open doors — doors to opportunities you may have never dreamed of. With knowledge, Anjali can choose her own path and build a better future for herself and for all of you."

Kamala looked down, unsure. "But the world outside our village feels distant and dangerous."

Raghav nodded. "That's why we want to work with you — to build a bridge between your traditions and the possibilities of tomorrow. Together."

Breaking Through

Later that evening, the team joined villagers around a crackling bonfire. The warm glow flickered across faces lined with hard work and hope.

Ravi, the elder teacher from their pilot, shared a story.

"When I first brought the app to my classroom, some elders said it would steal children's souls. But now, I see that it stirs their minds and hearts."

Deepa, a younger teacher, added, "The app helps me teach in ways I never imagined — but it's the children's laughter and curiosity that remind me why I chose this profession."

The villagers laughed, the tension easing with each shared story.

Anika noticed Kamala standing quietly at the edge, watching the flames dance.

"Kamala ji," she called softly. "What do you think now?"

Kamala hesitated, then said, "I'm still afraid. But when I see Anjali reading stories with a smile, maybe... maybe there is room for both the old and the new."

Leadership Under Fire

Back in Mumbai, the pressure weighed heavily on Raghav's shoulders. Investors demanded rapid progress; emails piled up with curt reminders and expectations.

One evening, Anika found him slumped at his desk, exhaustion etched deep into his features.

"You carry too much alone," she said softly.

He looked up, eyes shadowed. "Sometimes I wonder if this fight is bigger than I am."

Anika smiled gently. "You're not alone. And sometimes, breaking barriers takes more than strength — it takes patience and the courage to bend without breaking."

A New Dawn for Girls' Education

Weeks later, EduInnovate launched a pilot program focused specifically on girls. Tailored educational content, community workshops addressing safety and cultural concerns, and the involvement of women leaders from the villages themselves.

At the opening ceremony in Navapur, Aarav stood beside Raghav, holding a tablet and beaming with pride.

The villagers gathered in the schoolyard, their faces a mixture of hope and guarded optimism.

Raghav addressed the crowd. "Today, we take a step forward — not just in education, but in trust, respect, and understanding. Together, we can break barriers."

The applause was tentative at first, then grew strong.

As the sun set behind the hills, Raghav felt a fragile but undeniable promise of change blooming.

Chapter 10: Voices on the Threshold

The morning air was thick with the scent of wet earth, a reminder of the monsoon's recent visit to Mumbai. Inside the bustling EduInnovate office, sunlight filtered through the windows, casting warm patches on the worn wooden floor. The team moved with purpose — meetings to be held, calls to be made, and plans to be refined.

Raghav sat at the head of the table, a stack of proposals spread before him. His eyes, sharp and focused, scanned each line, seeking solutions that could propel their mission forward. The success in Navapur had energized the team, but the path ahead was still lined with obstacles.

Anika entered carrying a steaming cup of chai, her eyes bright. "There's news from the government office — the pilot program has been approved for expansion into three new districts."

Raghav's face broke into a rare smile. "That's the breakthrough we needed. But with scale comes complexity."

Priya nodded. "We need more trainers, more support staff, and stronger community engagement."

New Faces, New Challenges

The expanded program meant fresh faces joined the EduInnovate family. Among them was Sanjay, a young volunteer teacher from Pune, eager but inexperienced.

On his first day in one of the new villages, Sanjay was met with a wall of skepticism.

"Why should we trust some stranger from the city?" a local elder challenged him.

Sanjay swallowed his nerves and replied, "I'm here to learn from you and to share tools that can help your children dream bigger."

Days turned into weeks as Sanjay built trust through patience and respect. Slowly, barriers began to crumble.

A Spark in the Classroom

In a dusty schoolroom, Aarav, now a confident teenager, helped a group of girls navigate the new educational app.

"See here," he explained, pointing to the tablet screen, "this story teaches about courage and kindness."

One girl, Meena, raised her hand shyly. "Will this help me become a teacher someday?"

Aarav smiled. "It can help you be anything you want. This is just the beginning."

The Pulse of the Community

The team hosted village meetings where parents and elders voiced their hopes and fears. Some evenings were filled with laughter and shared meals; others, with heated debates about tradition and change.

Anika found herself bridging worlds, translating technical jargon into stories that resonated with the villagers' daily lives.

Inside the Government Halls

Meanwhile, Raghav navigated the corridors of power, advocating for policy changes to support digital education.

A tense meeting with Mr. Iyer and other officials tested his resolve.

"You need to show measurable results," Iyer insisted. "And ensure alignment with national standards."

Raghav nodded. "We are committed to transparency and collaboration. This is about investing in the future of our children."

The Personal Cost

As the work intensified, the personal lives of the team frayed at the edges.

Priya's nights were sleepless, tending to her ailing child.

Meera juggled family duties with her passion for teaching.

Anika missed her mother's birthday, caught in yet another field visit.

Raghav felt the weight of responsibility grow heavier with each passing day.

A Moment of Reflection

One quiet evening, Raghav stood on the office rooftop, gazing at the city's sprawling skyline.

Anika joined him, handing him a cup of tea.

"We're making progress," she said softly. "Slow, imperfect progress."

He smiled faintly. "The winds of change don't rush. They take their time, but they always arrive."

Together, they watched as the city lights blinked to life, a mosaic of dreams, struggles, and hope.

Chapter 11: Turning Tides

The first light of dawn stretched over the village of Navapur, filtering through the cracked wooden windows of the schoolhouse like delicate threads of hope. The scent of wet earth, freshly watered crops, and morning jasmine filled the air as children slowly filtered into the classroom, their faces a mixture of curiosity and nervous excitement.

Inside, the rows of old desks—scarred with years of use—stood in stark contrast to the sleek tablets resting on each one, a symbol of the change that was sweeping the village. Aarav, now taller and steadier in his demeanor, moved between the desks, patiently helping the youngest learners navigate the unfamiliar screens.

Raghav stood near the entrance, arms crossed, watching silently. The hum of soft voices, interspersed with laughter and gasps of surprise at the digital stories, filled the room. For a moment, the merging of tradition and technology seemed seamless—a quiet victory.

Then a sharp voice shattered the calm.

"Sir! Please, come quickly!"

It was Aarav, running toward Raghav, urgency shining in his eyes.

"What is it?" Raghav asked, his calm faltering.

"There's a group of parents gathered outside. They're upset—angry about the lessons the children are learning."

Raghav's stomach tightened. This was the resistance he knew was inevitable.

Outside the schoolhouse, a crowd had gathered. The air was thick with tension; voices rose and fell like waves crashing on rocky shores. Among the group stood Ganesh, an elder with a face creased by decades of hard labor and eyes fierce with concern.

"These lessons," Ganesh said, raising his voice so all could hear, "teach things that don't belong to our culture. Our children are forgetting the stories of their ancestors. How can that be right?"

A mother, wiping away tears, added, "My son came home asking questions I couldn't answer. He wonders why we don't follow the old ways anymore. I fear we are losing ourselves."

The murmurs grew louder, and several villagers nodded in agreement. For them, education was no longer just a tool for advancement—it was a threat to their identity.

Raghav stepped forward, trying to steady his voice. "I hear you. Change is difficult, and I understand your fears. But this program isn't about erasing who you are. It's about giving your children the tools to survive and succeed in a world that is changing rapidly."

Anika joined him, her expression soft but resolute. "We want to learn from you, not replace you. Tell us what you need to feel confident in this new journey."

One by one, voices rose and fell, sharing worries about safety, values, and the pace of change.

Kamala, standing quietly in the back, finally spoke. "I was afraid too. But when I see my daughter reading stories she never could before, when she dreams of being a teacher or an artist, I realize this is a gift."

Her words hung in the air, softening the anger.

Building bridges between the old and the new became the team's next mission.

Raghav proposed blending local folklore and traditions into the educational app—stories told in the mother tongue, lessons that celebrated local heroes and values alongside modern subjects.

Meera suggested hosting monthly community workshops. "Let the parents see what their children learn. Let them ask questions, share stories, and feel part of this change."

Over the next few weeks, the atmosphere began to shift. The app featured tales of Navapur's founding, songs sung by elders, and lessons that linked technology with culture.

The villagers slowly moved from suspicion to cautious

curiosity.

At one such evening workshop, laughter filled the air as parents, elders, and children gathered around warm fires. Aarav, standing before a circle of wide-eyed kids, narrated an interactive folk tale from the app.

"Once upon a time, in these very hills, lived a brave girl who taught her village to read the stars," he said, his voice animated.

The children's eyes sparkled, and even the adults leaned in closer.

Meanwhile, in Mumbai, Raghav and Anika prepared for a crucial presentation to government officials.

"We need your support," Raghav said firmly during the meeting. "What we're building isn't just about technology or education — it's about honoring traditions while empowering the next generation."

Mr. Iyer, a senior bureaucrat, nodded thoughtfully. "Your approach shows promise. But remember, scalability and measurable impact will determine long-term success."

Raghav nodded. "We understand. That's why we're committed to transparency and continuous learning."

But success came with personal costs.

Priya, exhausted from balancing her role as

EduInnovate's lead researcher and caring for her sick child, sat silently during meetings, eyes heavy.

Meera juggled late-night lessons and early mornings in the field, all while caring for her aging parents.

Anika missed family celebrations and birthdays, her heart aching with the sacrifices she made.

Raghav himself sometimes felt overwhelmed, the weight of thousands of children's futures pressing on his shoulders.

One evening, after a long day, Raghav stood on the rooftop terrace of their office building, gazing out over the sprawling cityscape.

Anika joined him quietly, handing over a cup of warm tea.

"We're making progress," she whispered, her voice calm.

Raghav sighed. "Slow, imperfect progress. But progress all the same."

"The winds of change," she said, "don't blow violently. They arrive softly, but they leave lasting marks."

Together, they watched as the city's lights blinked awake—a mosaic of dreams, struggles, and hope stretching as far as the eye could see.

The tides were turning, but the journey had only just begun

Chapter 12:
Seeds of Doubt

The monsoon had passed, leaving behind fields thick with promise and roads caked with stubborn, drying mud. In the village of Devlipur—a newer expansion site for EduInnovate—the rain had washed clean the cracked walls of the schoolhouse, but not the unease that now simmered beneath the surface of progress.

Inside the temporary learning center built from bamboo and tin sheets, the air buzzed with the hum of learning. Children sat cross-legged on mats, eyes locked on tablets that glowed like little stars in the dim morning light. On the screen danced a tale of a girl from Jharkhand who used math to redesign her village's water system—a story that blended fiction with possibility.

But outside, behind the smiles, whispers had begun to take root. Rumors. Mistrust. Unspoken fears that the change sweeping through Devlipur carried a silent cost.

Raghav leaned back in the rickety plastic chair set up near the school's entrance, rubbing the bridge of his nose with his fingers. He had arrived early that morning, hoping to check on the progress of their newest site in person. Instead, he found a staff exhausted, a team divided, and parents lingering at the fringes of the schoolyard, watching—always watching—but no longer speaking to the teachers with the same warmth.

Priya emerged from inside, her thick black braid swinging as she walked toward him.

"They're pulling back," she said bluntly, her voice flat with fatigue. "Attendance dropped by thirty percent this week."

"Why?" Raghav asked. He already feared the answer.

"Some say their children are disrespecting elders. That they speak of cities and jobs and don't want to farm anymore. Others..." she hesitated, lowering her voice. "There's a rumor that the tablets have cameras. That we're... spying on them. Sending data to foreign governments."

Raghav stared at her in disbelief. "What? That's absurd."

Priya nodded. "Absurd, yes. But belief isn't always built on logic. It's built on trust. And something's broken here."

Later that afternoon, a tense community meeting was called.

Dozens gathered under the shade of a neem tree near the temple steps. The school team sat across from them, a low folding table between them. Anika arrived just in time, brushing dust from her kurta, her face weary but resolute.

Ganesh, an elder from a neighboring village, spoke first. "We welcomed your team. We saw the good. But now our children mock our ways. My grandson told me he'd rather go to the city and 'code.' He said farming was backward. That came from your app."

"It's not from our app," Anika said carefully. "It may be from his own dreams. Dreams you helped plant by letting him learn."

A woman in a bright pink saree stood up. "And what if those dreams take him away? What if we give them wings and they never come back?"

Raghav took a deep breath. "I hear your pain. I really do. But what if you give them wings... and they fly back with seeds?"

Silence fell. His words lingered in the air.

That night, Raghav sat with Anika by the well behind the school, the distant chirp of insects rising like a lullaby from the fields.

"Do you ever feel like we're losing them?" she asked quietly.

"Yes," he replied. "But I think we're also finding something else."

Anika turned to look at him. "What's that?"

"The truth," he said. "About what change really costs. And who pays the price first."

She didn't speak for a long while. Then, almost a whisper, she said, "Maybe that's why it's called sacrifice.

Morning broke with a sharpness that felt unnatural — not because of the weather, which remained warm and forgiving, but because something had shifted in the spirit of the place. The cheerful, chaotic energy that usually echoed through the schoolyard had faded. In its place was a quiet, heavy stillness.

Raghav woke early, as he always did, but today there was no rush to lace his shoes or sip tea with urgency. The rhythm of the day had slowed, and he could feel it in his bones. He stepped outside and saw Aarav seated on a low wall, quietly feeding a stray dog with a roti torn into pieces.

"You're up early," Raghav said gently.

Aarav nodded but didn't speak. There was a darkness in his eyes — not sadness exactly, but something adjacent. Doubt.

Raghav sat beside him.

"What's going on, Aarav?"

The boy stared at the ground, fingers tightening around the last piece of bread.

"People are saying... we're not real. That this learning is a trick. That we'll forget our parents. That we'll turn into strangers."

He glanced up, and the pain in his voice was unmistakable. "Is that true? Will I forget them, Sir?"

Raghav's throat tightened. How could he explain the world to someone caught in its in-between?

"You'll never forget them," Raghav said after a pause. "Not if you keep your heart open. You're learning, not leaving. But it feels like leaving to them. Because they don't understand where you're going."

Inside the schoolroom, tension brewed in the team as well. Priya had been quiet all morning, her eyes shadowed by sleepless nights and growing anxiety. During the morning strategy meeting, she finally snapped.

"We should pause the expansion," she said, her voice clipped. "Something's wrong here, and pushing ahead without understanding it is reckless."

Anika frowned. "We're already behind schedule. We've committed to launching in two more villages by next month. If we delay—"

"If we delay," Priya interrupted, "we might actually *listen* for once instead of just reacting."

The room fell silent.

Raghav looked between the two women. This was no longer just about educational models or digital inclusion. This was about emotional fatigue, cultural misfires, and the limits of idealism.

"We need to breathe," he said softly. "All of us."

That afternoon, Raghav went door to door through Devlipur, alone.

He didn't bring a tablet. No banners, no presentations, no pitch. Just a notebook and his ears.

He stopped by the carpenter's house. A man named Babu opened the door, cautious but not unkind.

"I came to listen," Raghav said.

Inside, they shared a glass of buttermilk while Babu spoke about his concerns.

"It's not that I don't want my daughter to learn," he said. "I just want to know she'll still sing the songs her mother taught her. That she'll still come home after college and sit under this roof."

"She will," Raghav replied.

"How can you know that?"

"I can't," Raghav admitted. "But I can promise that if she does leave, it will be because she's following her calling — not because she's running from you."

Later, Raghav found himself at the edge of a farm where a group of women were collecting mustard leaves.

One of them, Parvati, pointed at him with her sickle. "You're the tech man, aren't you?"

Raghav smiled. "So they say."

She narrowed her eyes. "My niece says she wants to be a 'robot scientist' now. Can you tell me what that even means?"

He laughed, shaking his head. "Honestly? Sometimes I don't even know. But if she learns enough, maybe one day she'll come back and build a machine that helps with harvest. Or cures crop diseases. Or... just teaches the next girl to dream like her."

Parvati paused, then handed him a small bunch of leaves. "Then teach her well. But tell her not to forget how to cook saag."

Back at the school, a decision was made to create a community council — an official voice for the villagers in the program's future.

At the first meeting, elders, parents, and even teenagers sat together for the first time. Questions were raised. Doubts were aired. Stories were shared.

By the end of the meeting, something subtle but powerful had shifted.

They weren't enemies anymore. They were participants.

That night, under the stars, Anika found Raghav sitting alone, knees tucked to his chest, watching the sky.

"Do you think we'll ever be fully accepted?" she asked.

"No," he said. "And maybe we shouldn't be."

She tilted her head. "Why not?"

"Because if we're fully accepted, it means we've stopped challenging them. And if they stop challenging us, it means we've become too comfortable."

Anika leaned her head against his shoulder.

"Still," she said, "a little comfort would be nice."

He chuckled softly. "Just a little."

The week wore on like a song stuck between verses—aching for resolution, yet unwilling to move forward.

The village had quieted in a way that wasn't peaceful, but tense. Eyes lingered too long. Conversations halted when a teacher passed. Even the children had begun to mirror the silence. That frightened Anika the most. Not the skepticism of the elders, not the slander whispered in corners—but the stillness of the children who once erupted with stories and laughter. That was the sound of doubt taking root.

Then, it happened.

A boy named *Mannu*—sharp, curious, with a hunger for knowledge that outpaced his years—collapsed during class.

Not physically, but emotionally. One moment he was answering questions about a solar project, the next he was curled into himself, sobbing uncontrollably.

"No more questions!" he screamed. "No more!"

The room froze. Priya dropped her tablet, rushing to him, but he flinched.

"They hate me!" he cried. "My father says I'm not his son anymore! That I've been changed!"

Raghav, who had been in the back grading a peer-learning rubric, stepped forward, his chest aching.

"Mannu," he said softly, kneeling beside him, "your father is afraid. That's not the same as hate."

"He said I speak like a stranger. That I think I'm better. I don't! I just wanted to show him what I built. But he slapped me."

No one spoke. Even the youngest children understood, in that moment, that the line between learning and loneliness was perilously thin.

That night, the team gathered in their makeshift staff room—a bamboo shed lined with papers and old chalkboards.

The energy was brittle.

"We can't keep doing this," Priya said, arms crossed, eyes burning. "It's not just Mannu. It's happening everywhere. We're unravelling kids from their families. Their *identities*."

"We're giving them tools," Anika countered. "The world is changing whether this village wants it to or not."

"And what happens when a twelve-year-old wants a world their father doesn't understand? When home becomes a place they're no longer welcome?"

No one replied.

In the silence that followed, Aarav—usually quiet during meetings—spoke up.

"I saw Mannu sitting near the old banyan tree tonight. Alone. Drawing circuits in the dirt with a stick. He's still dreaming. He just doesn't know if it's allowed anymore."

Raghav looked around the room. "That's the real battle," he said. "Not education. *Permission to dream.*"

The next day, Raghav visited Mannu's home.

It was a low hut on the edge of the fields, a place that smelled of mustard oil and drying grain. Mannu's father, **Ramdas**, sat outside stringing together bundles of kindling.

He didn't look up.

"You've come to shame me?" Ramdas asked bitterly. "To say I don't love my son?"

"No," Raghav said calmly. "I've come to understand what scares you."

Ramdas paused. His fingers slowed. "He used to run to me when he solved something. Now he runs to that... that screen."

"Because it listens," Raghav replied. "And maybe you stopped."

That stung. Ramdas looked away. "He asked me about solar panels. What do I know of such things? I dig earth. I don't build skies."

"You built *him*," Raghav said gently.

Ramdas broke then—not into tears, but into something deeper. A silence soaked in shame.

"I never thought my child's brightness would make me feel so... dim."

Raghav sat beside him. "Then learn beside him. Ask questions. Be curious again. He doesn't need you to be perfect. Just present."

That evening, in the learning center, Mannu walked in late. The children looked up, expecting him to sit quietly at the back.

Instead, he pulled out his tablet, walked straight to the board, and opened a project design for a water filter he'd created using sand and charcoal.

"My father helped me gather the materials," he said. "He says he wants to build one for our well."

No one clapped. No one needed to.

Because in that moment, a truth settled over the room like sunlight through a cracked roof:

Trust, once lost, could be rebuilt—not through proof, but through participation.

Later, as the sun melted behind the mango trees, Anika found Raghav sitting alone again, this time on the school's rooftop, legs swinging over the edge.

"You look less like a visionary tonight," she teased.

He smiled weakly. "And more like what?"

"Like someone who's finally starting to *feel* the weight of the vision."

He nodded. "It's heavier than I thought."

"Still want to carry it?"

"Yes," he said without hesitation. "But I think... we need more hands."

She sat beside him. "And more hearts."

Chapter 13:
The Storm Beneath Still Waters

The stillness of early morning in Dharigunj was deceiving. The air, though cool, felt dense — as though it carried unsaid words, withheld tears, and a tremor of change too subtle for the eye but impossible for the heart to ignore.

Inside the school, Raghav stood at the blackboard, staring not at the lessons written there, but at the peeling edges of the paint. It had become a metaphor of sorts — knowledge layered, cracked, imperfect, yet refusing to be erased.

The children filtered in slowly that day. Their footsteps hesitant. Their voices lower than usual. Meera, always first, sat in silence with her hands clenched into fists. Aarav, the one who usually sparked trouble with his clever retorts, looked lost in a fog of thought. Something had shifted.

Raghav knew better than to probe too soon.

"Let's begin," he said, his voice as calm as the room was charged. "Not with math today. Not even language. But something else."

He erased the board.

"What does silence mean to you?"

The children stared at him.

"Is it absence?" he continued. "Or presence? Is silence what we choose, or what we are forced into?"

Aarav raised his hand slowly. "Sometimes silence is because... no one is listening anyway."

Meera followed. "Or because if you speak, someone will tell you you're wrong. Again."

Tara, barely above a whisper, said, "Silence is safer. You can't fail if you don't try."

Raghav let their words sit like pebbles dropped into still water. Each rippled into the others.

Outside, the clouds began gathering. The wind picked up with the nervous energy of something unresolved.

"Let's write," Raghav said. "Not what you think. But what you've never dared say aloud."

They hesitated. Pencils hovered.

Then one by one, they wrote. Not essays, not assignments, but confessions. Hopes too delicate for daylight. Fears they hadn't known how to name.

Meera wrote about the night her father had shouted at her for staying late at school. How he had ripped her textbook and told her no husband would ever care what she knew.

Aarav wrote about the weight of being told he was lazy, stupid, destined to be nothing. How he had started to believe it.

Tara wrote about her mother weeping when her older brother dropped out to work at a brick kiln. And how she pretended not to hear.

The storm outside grew louder. Thunder cracked not far off. Raghav stood still, holding the moment like glass in his hands.

"You are not wrong for feeling these things," he said softly. "You are not weak because you carry them. You are stronger than anyone sees. Even you."

The power went out. Rain slammed the windows. The wind howled through the doorways like a cry set free.

Yet inside, a strange peace settled.

They sat together — not teacher and student, not poor and privileged — but as a circle of survivors. Not of war, but of silence.

After class, Raghav found Anika outside, drenched from checking on the supply shed.

"You look like you tried to wrestle the monsoon," he said, offering her a towel.

She chuckled, but her eyes were tired.

"They've started again," she said.

He didn't need to ask who.

"Village whispers. That we're giving these kids dreams too big for their lives. That we're turning daughters into rebels and sons into... strangers."

He sat beside her on the stone ledge. The rain softened into a curtain.

"They're scared," he said. "Because when a child begins to question, the world around them must answer."

She turned to him, her voice a mix of anger and exhaustion. "But we're not asking them to revolt. Just... to see differently."

"And that," he said, "is the most frightening thing of all."

Later that evening, a knock came on the school door. A man stood outside — lean, weather-worn, eyes too old for his age.

Meera's father.

"I came to see what she's learning," he said, not with anger, but with curiosity that had cracked through pride.

Raghav welcomed him in.

Meera was at her desk, helping Tara write a poem.

Her father watched quietly.

"Can she really do this?" he asked. "Be more?"

"She already is," Raghav said. "You just have to see her as she's becoming — not as what you feared she would be."

There was no answer. But something flickered in the man's eyes — recognition, maybe. Or regret.

The next morning, Meera walked into class with a notebook — new, untouched. She smiled at Raghav.

"My father bought it for me."

It was the first time anyone had ever given her something for learning — not to stop her, but to support her.

That small gesture felt larger than any policy, any speech.

Outside, the rain had stopped. The soil, drenched and fertile, waited for seeds to be planted.

And inside, something had already begun to grow.

Chapter 14:
The Firefly Paradox

Night draped itself slowly over the village, not with sudden darkness but with a gentle hush, like the soft closing of an ancient book. The last rays of the sun disappeared behind the distant hills, casting long shadows across the cracked mud paths and thatched roofs. The sky bloomed with stars, silent witnesses to the secrets the earth kept and the stories it told.

Under the great neem tree by the school courtyard, a handful of fireflies flickered—a scattered constellation of tiny lights blinking in and out like hesitant hopes. The children's laughter had faded hours ago, but somewhere deep inside the quiet, the village seemed to breathe a little easier than it had the night before.

Inside the modest school building, Raghav sat by his open window. His notebook lay on the wooden sill, pages fluttering slightly in the evening breeze. But no words came. Just the soft rustle of paper and the steady pulse of his breath. He watched the fireflies and wondered if he was as elusive as their glow—visible only at night, fading with the dawn.

His mind replayed the day's events.

Across the courtyard, in the learning center, Priya sat on

the floor surrounded by a scatter of papers and open books. She wasn't marking tests or planning lessons. Instead, she stared at the wall, her mind tangled in thoughts she hadn't yet dared to voice aloud.

When Anika entered quietly, Priya didn't look up.

"We haven't talked," Anika said softly.

"No," Priya answered after a long pause.

Anika crossed the room and sat down opposite her. "If you're leaving, tell me."

Priya's fingers trembled as she folded a paper crane. "I'm thinking about it."

"Why now?" Anika's voice was fragile, almost breaking.

"Because I don't know if I still belong here. Or maybe... if this place still belongs to me."

Anika swallowed the lump in her throat. "We're growing, Priya. Together."

Priya's eyes finally met hers, glistening with unshed tears. "Are we? Or are we just running faster to escape the very people we promised to serve?"

Anika reached out instinctively, but Priya pulled back. "I wanted to build with the village, not just for it. But lately, I feel like we're racing to impress outsiders. Metrics, funding, scalability... It's like the soul is being squeezed out."

Anika nodded, words caught in her chest.

Priya exhaled deeply, voice barely above a whisper. "We can't lose the quiet strength—the patient roots that hold this soil together."

Outside, the village was preparing for another night. Women collected water from the well, sharing news and worries in hushed tones. The men sat near the tea stall, debating politics and progress. But beneath these everyday rituals, something subtle was shifting—a cautious curiosity that hadn't existed before.

Raghav left his window and walked through the dusty streets, feeling the weight of both hope and uncertainty pressing on his shoulders.

He passed the grain shop, where an elderly man was teaching a boy to count coins, patient and kind. The child fumbled, then smiled proudly at getting the count right.

"No tablets. No apps," Raghav thought. "Just simple lessons, slow and steady."

He made a note in his journal: *"Not all seeds need our hands. Some just need room to grow."*

The next morning, a sleek black car rumbled into the village, stirring up clouds of dust and whispers.

Out stepped Mr. Joshi, the potential donor, his polished shoes at odds with the cracked mud beneath them. His sharp eyes scanned the school buildings and the scattered children.

"So this is where all the 'innovation' happens?" His tone was polite but edged with skepticism.

"Yes," Raghav replied, stepping forward.

Joshi looked around, frowning. "Where's the digital lab? The high-tech classrooms?"

"We blend technology with tradition," Raghav said carefully. "Solar panels, recycled materials, hands-on projects."

Joshi's smile didn't reach his eyes. "Scalability requires structure. Clear hierarchies. Measurable outcomes."

Anika bristled but stayed silent.

Joshi continued, "Without those, this remains a charming pilot, not a model to scale."

Later that evening, Joshi sat with the team in the dim light of the staff room.

"I admire your passion," he began, "but passion isn't enough. We need data. Numbers. Growth charts."

Raghav's eyes locked with Joshi's.

"Children are not data points."

Joshi chuckled darkly. "Everything can be quantified."

"Not everything should be."

The room grew tense.

After the meeting, the team dispersed under a sky heavy

with stars.

Anika stood on the rooftop, lighting paper lanterns—hundreds of them. They floated softly into the night air, fragile beacons of hope and resistance.

Mannu joined her, holding a lantern hesitantly.

"Sir, what if all this is forgotten someday?" he asked quietly.

Raghav stepped beside them, watching the glowing orbs drift upward.

"We won't be forgotten," he said. "Because we lived it. And what we live leaves traces — sometimes invisible, but always lasting."

The lanterns drifted higher, like fireflies escaping the darkness.

A river of light against the night sky.

As the village settled into sleep, Priya sat alone beneath the neem tree.

She whispered to the stars, "Maybe this is the paradox. Like fireflies, we shine brightest when we choose to be seen—but only when the night is dark enough to hold us."

And somewhere in the stillness, the village held its breath—waiting to see if the light would last.

Chapter 15: Shadows in the Light

The dawn spilled softly through the cracked wooden shutters, stretching thin fingers of gold over the humble schoolroom. The air was thick with a quiet tension, a weight that seemed to press against the walls and seep into the dust-covered books and worn wooden desks. The village, usually so alive at sunrise with the chatter of children and the rhythmic thumping of daily chores, was subdued.

Inside, Priya sat motionless, her fingers clenched tightly around a piece of paper. The edges were crumpled, as if they had been folded and unfolded countless times in restless hands. The words on the page were stark and final:

I resign.

The letter felt like an anchor dropped deep into the heart of the school. It pulled at everything around it, creating ripples of uncertainty and sorrow.

When Raghav arrived later that morning, the usual warmth of the courtyard was absent. The laughter of children was subdued, replaced by whispers that quickly stopped when he approached. He noticed Anika standing near the old banyan tree, her shoulders slumped, eyes shadowed with worry. Mannu lingered nearby, avoiding eye contact.

"Where's Priya?" Raghav asked quietly.

Anika's voice trembled as she answered, "She left last night. Without saying goodbye."

The words hit Raghav like a sudden chill. His chest tightened as if the breath had been squeezed out.

"Why?" he asked, desperate for an explanation.

"She said the work is no longer what she signed up for," Anika whispered. "She feels the soul is slipping through our fingers, replaced by deadlines and expectations. She said we're losing the very heart of this place."

Raghav closed his eyes and exhaled slowly. The absence of Priya, once a pillar of their efforts, left a hollow ache.

The rest of the day passed in a blur for Raghav. Meetings felt hollow. The sound of children's voices no longer lifted his spirits. He found himself retreating beneath the neem tree at dusk, notebook open but blank.

He stared at the fluttering fireflies, their soft lights blinking in the growing darkness, wondering if they carried more wisdom than he did.

Suddenly, a slow shuffle interrupted his thoughts.

An elderly man appeared, leaning heavily on a wooden cane, his steps measured but steady. His face was a map of wrinkles, each line telling a story of hardship, laughter, and endurance.

"Raghav?" the man's voice was gentle but firm.

"Yes," Raghav replied, startled by the presence.

"I am Das," the man said, "your grandfather's old friend."

Recognition flickered across Raghav's face. His grandfather had often spoken of Das, the village elder who had been a silent guardian of their traditions.

"What brings you here?" Raghav asked, curiosity mingling with a strange sense of destiny.

Das smiled, his eyes shining with unspoken knowledge. "I have come to share what your father never could. Secrets buried beneath this soil, stories waiting to be uncovered."

Raghav's heart beat faster. The promise of hidden truths stirred something deep within him.

Over the course of many hours, Das unfolded tales of the village's past — sacrifices made in silence, dreams that had flickered and almost died, and a legacy that wove through generations like an invisible thread.

"The light you chase," Das said, voice dropping to a whisper, "is not new. It is the same flame your ancestors carried. It has been passed down, through hardships and hopes, waiting for you to kindle it anew."

Raghav listened, each story igniting a fierce resolve inside him. He realized that the struggle wasn't his alone — it was a continuation of a timeless battle between preservation and progress, tradition and change.

Meanwhile, the tension within the school grew. Mr. Joshi's visits became more frequent, his demands more insistent.

"We need to see results," Joshi said sharply during a meeting, "clear metrics, expansion plans, a hierarchy that ensures accountability."

Anika challenged him softly, "And if the heart of our work cannot be measured by numbers? What then?"

Joshi's eyes narrowed. "Then you are not ready for growth."

Arguments flared. The team found themselves at a crossroads between maintaining their values and adapting to survive.

That night, beneath a canopy of stars, Raghav and Anika stood on the rooftop, releasing hundreds of paper lanterns into the sky.

The lanterns floated upwards, tiny flames battling the dark, carrying silent prayers and hopes.

Mannu watched in awe, breaking the silence with a quiet question.

"Sir, what if no one remembers this place? This struggle?"

Raghav's eyes followed the lanterns drifting higher.

"Sometimes, the brightest lights are those that burn unseen, in the darkest nights," he said softly. "Our legacy is not always in grand monuments but in the lives we touch and the hope we spark."

The lanterns shimmered, like fireflies released from captivity, a delicate rebellion against the night.

Later, alone under the neem tree, Priya's whispered words carried into the night air.

"Maybe this is the paradox of light. Like fireflies, we are most beautiful when we choose to be seen... but only when the darkness is deep enough to hold us."

The village, in its quiet slumber, held its breath, waiting to see if that light would endure.

Chapter 16: The Crossroads of Conviction

The mist clung to the village like a soft veil, blurring the edges of trees and rooftops, wrapping the earth in a fragile calm. But beneath this quiet morning surface, a storm brewed — not of wind or rain, but of doubt, hope, and conviction.

Raghav's footsteps echoed down the narrow path leading to the school, each step heavy with the weight of responsibility. His mind replayed the difficult conversations of the past weeks — the clashes with Joshi, Priya's sudden departure, the weary faces of his team. The pressure to scale, to grow faster, to show tangible results was mounting, yet with every demand, the essence of their mission seemed to slip further away.

He entered the conference room, where Anika was already waiting, surrounded by scattered papers, charts, and faded photographs from the village's past. Mannu leaned against the wall, eyes downcast but alert.

Raghav exhaled deeply, letting the silence settle between them before speaking.

"We're standing at a fork in the road," he said, voice low but resolute. "Joshi wants numbers. Growth. Expansion. But at what cost? If we lose the heart, what's left to grow?"

Anika nodded slowly, her eyes meeting his with steady resolve. "We can't deny the need for progress. The children deserve better opportunities than we had. But that progress can't come from a template or a spreadsheet. It has to be rooted here — in this community, this culture, these stories."

Mannu shifted, finally raising his voice. "Is it possible to balance both? To keep what makes us special, and still reach out wider?"

Raghav smiled faintly, the tension easing for a moment. "That's what we have to find out."

As the sun rose higher, the school's courtyard filled with voices — villagers, teachers, and students gathering beneath the sprawling branches of the banyan tree. The circle was a mix of hope and frustration, tradition and uncertainty.

Raghav stepped forward, clearing his throat. "This school is more than a building. It's a living promise to all of us. But we cannot do this alone. Your voices, your stories, your hopes — they must guide us."

The village elder, Ramdas, who had seen decades pass like seasons, raised his hand. "We want our children to fly higher than we ever could. But if the price is losing ourselves, what remains?"

Anika responded gently, "We are not here to replace who we are, but to help who we can become — together."

A teacher, Meera, added, "We need education that honors both the past and the future. A bridge, not a barrier."

The conversation deepened. Voices rose and fell, ideas clashing and coalescing like a storm and its clearing sky. Some villagers worried about rapid change; others embraced it with cautious optimism.

Raghav listened, heart pounding. In that circle, he saw the future not as a fixed path but as a river — ever-changing, shaped by the stones and currents within it.

Evening fell soft and slow. On the rooftop overlooking the village, the sky blazed with color — oranges fading to purples, stars waiting their turn to shine.

Raghav and Anika sat side by side, the cool breeze carrying the scent of earth and wood smoke.

"We've been fighting battles outside," Anika murmured, "but the real fight is inside us — who we want to be, what we will stand for."

Raghav looked at her, gratitude and hope mingling in his gaze. "Leading isn't about knowing the answers. It's about holding space for the questions."

Anika smiled, her fingers brushing his. "And we have each other."

The first stars blinked awake, silent witnesses to a promise forged between two hearts and a restless village.

Days unfolded in a rhythm both familiar and new. The school began to shift, adapting with careful steps.

New programs were co-created with elders and children, blending technology with tradition. Science lessons included stories of the village's medicinal plants; history classes told tales of forgotten heroes.

Raghav stood before a circle of eager children one afternoon, holding a simple solar panel.

"Why does the sun give us power?" a small girl asked, eyes wide with curiosity.

"Because," Raghav replied, "even when clouds hide it, the sun never stops shining. Like hope — it's always there, even if we can't always see it."

A chorus of "Wow!" followed.

Outside the school gates, the village stirred with new energy. Markets buzzed, elders shared stories on benches, children raced down dusty lanes — their laughter a bright thread weaving through the air.

But Joshi's shadow loomed. His messages grew sterner.

"We cannot delay progress," he warned in a meeting. "Without numbers, there is no funding. Without funding, no future."

The tension returned, but this time tempered by the village's newfound unity.

Raghav stood firm. "Progress without soul is a hollow

victory. We will measure success by the lives we change, not just the data we produce."

One night, under the sprawling neem tree, fireflies flickered softly like tiny stars brought to earth.

Raghav and Anika sat quietly, their thoughts heavy but hopeful.

"I sometimes wonder," Anika said, "if light born from shadows is the brightest of all."

Raghav nodded. "We are fireflies in the dark. Small, fragile, but luminous."

Their hands met, fingers intertwining in a silent vow.

The village slept beneath a canopy of dreams. And in the quiet glow of countless tiny lights, a new chapter began — fragile, uncertain, but alive with possibility.

Chapter 17: Tectonic Shifts

The village woke slowly beneath the fragile light of dawn. Mist curled over the riverbanks, reluctant to yield to the warming sun, while the faint scent of jasmine lingered in the cool morning air. Inside the old school's weathered walls, a different kind of awakening stirred. It was a hum of purpose, a stirring in the hearts of those who had gathered to imagine the future.

Raghav stepped onto the cracked stone pathway leading into the courtyard where the teachers had already assembled. The faded paint of the school sign seemed brighter today, almost as if it too sensed the weight of what was to come. His footsteps echoed softly, mingling with the distant crowing of roosters and the clatter of morning chores in the village.

"Thank you all for coming," he began, voice steady but warm. "We stand at a crossroads. What we decide now will shape the future of this school—and the very soul of our village."

Anika, standing beside him with her quiet confidence, added, "We must ask ourselves what kind of progress truly matters. Is success simply numbers on a page? Or is it something deeper—something that reaches into the heart of who we are?"

The teachers shifted uneasily, caught between hope and hesitation. Sunil, the math teacher whose graying hair spoke of years spent in this very classroom, finally spoke. "The world beyond our hills changes with such speed it leaves me dizzy. Sometimes I wonder if we're standing still."

Mannu, the youngest among them and still finding his place, raised a hand. "Maybe standing still isn't so bad. Maybe it means we're holding on to what's important."

Raghav smiled gently. "Change is coming, yes, but it must be guided by our values—the stories we tell ourselves, the dreams that live in our hearts. This is our home. We decide what kind of future it will hold."

Outside, the village stirred. Barefoot children ran through puddles, their laughter carrying the pure joy of youth. Elders gathered near the well, sharing news and memories with voices low but full of meaning. Amid the everyday rhythms, an undercurrent of tension lingered—the pressure of expectations from outside authorities, the absence of Priya's steady presence, and the delicate balance between tradition and transformation.

As Raghav caught his reflection in a cracked mirror inside the school, he saw tired eyes but also fierce determination. "This is our moment," he whispered to himself.

Weeks passed, and the school courtyard blossomed into a place of vibrant activity and deep conversations. Villagers, once hesitant, now gathered more frequently—farmers, shopkeepers, mothers, fathers, and elders—drawn by the vision Raghav and Anika nurtured but also fearful of the unknown.

One afternoon, beneath the sprawling branches of the village's ancient banyan tree, a meeting was called that would test the fragile unity they had built. The air was heavy with anticipation and the scent of damp earth after a passing shower.

Raghav stood before the crowd, his voice calm but urgent. "We are at a turning point. The future of our children depends on the choices we make today."

Ramdas, the village elder whose face was etched with decades of hardship and hope, spoke with quiet authority. "Our village has survived droughts, floods, and famine, but this change you speak of—it challenges the very essence of who we are."

Anika added, "Progress is not the enemy. It's about honoring where we come from while opening doors to new possibilities. We must learn to walk both paths."

Voices rose—some fearful of losing identity, others eager for opportunity. Bhavna, the fierce shopkeeper, questioned, "Will our children forget their roots in this rush to modernize?"

Ramesh, a young father, countered, "If we don't prepare them for the wider world, how can we protect them from being left behind?"

The debate swirled like the wind itself, a mix of passion, fear, and hope.

That night, as stars blinked silently above, Raghav and Anika sat beneath a single lantern's glow. "How do we lead when the ground beneath us feels so unsteady?" Anika's voice was barely a whisper.

"We hold fast," Raghav replied, eyes on the dark sky. "Not by clinging to the past, but by weaving it into the future."

Slowly, the winds of change began to stir not only in words but in action.

Mannu took initiative, organizing a community garden project where children and elders planted together—blending traditional farming wisdom with new techniques. The children's laughter echoed as they dug into the soil, while elders shared stories of rain gods and harvest seasons. The garden became a living classroom, a symbol of roots and growth entwined.

Anika introduced evening storytelling sessions, inviting elders to share folklore that wove lessons of resilience, kindness, and curiosity into the fabric of education.

Raghav championed openness, inviting villagers into school planning meetings, turning suspicion into shared ownership.

But challenges remained. Joshi's letters and visits reminded them of the harsh realities beyond their village—demanding quick results and strict numbers that sometimes felt at odds with their vision.

Raghav kept Priya's last letter close—a mixture of sorrow and hope. "We carry her fight forward," he vowed.

Yet, not everyone embraced these changes. A faction within the village grew wary, fearing loss of identity and control. Rumors spread like wildfire, trust fractured, and old wounds bled anew.

During a particularly heated meeting, voices clashed fiercely. Tears were shed; anger flared. Raghav stepped forward, calm amid the storm. "We cannot build a future on fear and division. Our strength lies in unity—honoring the past while embracing what's to come."

The crowd grew silent, tension still thick, but cracks of hope glimmered.

That night, beneath the neem tree, Raghav sought strength from the whispered voices of ancestors. "We are the forge," he thought. "Tempered by fire, shaped by struggle."

With the dawn came renewal. The school thrived not only as a place of learning but as the heart of community life. Children learned not just facts, but the meaning of courage, compassion, and belonging.

Anika's words rang clear in the halls. "This is more than education—it is the weaving of many threads, old and new, into a tapestry stronger than any one of us alone."

Raghav watched the children—faces alight with curiosity and hope—and felt a swelling pride.

Joshi returned, clipboard in hand, but his eyes softened as he saw transformation not only in structures but in spirits.

"Perhaps," he said slowly, "progress is more than numbers. It is life itself."

Under the banyan tree, the village gathered, lanterns lifted high—a beacon of resilience and light in the ever-turning wind.

Raghav looked toward the rising sun, its golden rays casting warmth and promise over the hills. The journey was far from over, but the path was clear.

"We are on the path," he thought, heart steady. "And the journey has only just begun."

Chapter 18:
The Echoes of Yesterday

The village stirred awake beneath a sky that slowly melted from inky midnight to a delicate hue of pale orange, signaling the beginning of another day. The usual chorus of roosters crowing, goats bleating, and children's playful shouts echoed across the narrow lanes and terraced fields. The scent of wet earth mixed with jasmine and the faint aroma of cooking fires whispered stories of life's eternal rhythm. Yet beneath the gentle murmur of routine, a tension hummed—a subtle, almost imperceptible vibration of uncertainty that threaded through the heart of every villager.

Raghav stood silently at the edge of the school courtyard, eyes tracing the movements of the children as they ran and tumbled with boundless energy. Their faces, flushed with excitement, mirrored the endless possibilities that education promised—but his own heart bore a heavier weight. Change was not always as swift and simple as children's laughter, and he sensed the fragile balance of hope and fear hanging in the air like an unspoken question.

Inside the school, Anika moved with purpose, rearranging the worn wooden desks into a wide circle.

The room had a fresh scent of chalk dust and newly polished floors, but more importantly, it carried the promise of new ways—new methods that sought to ignite curiosity rather than mere memorization. The circle was not just a seating arrangement; it was a symbol of unity, equality, and the power of shared stories.

The children trickled in, their chatter softening as they took their places. Some whispered excitedly, their faces alight with the anticipation of a different kind of lesson. Others were more reserved, unsure of what was to come. Ramdas, the village elder whose skin was a map of decades weathered by sun and sorrow, entered quietly. His presence commanded respect, his calm voice a thread that wove together generations.

"Today, we talk about our stories," Ramdas began, settling into the circle. "Not the stories from books, but the stories that live in our hearts—the echoes of yesterday. They remind us of who we are."

The children's eyes widened, and even the youngest leaned forward, eager to listen. Raghav and Anika exchanged a knowing glance. This was the moment where education met tradition, where knowledge became a bridge rather than a barrier.

"Long ago," Ramdas continued, "before many of you were born, this village faced hardships that tested the very soul of its people. There were seasons of drought so severe the rivers ran dry and the fields cracked beneath the scorching sun. But it was also a time of great courage."

A hand shot up. It belonged to Meera, a curious girl with bright eyes and a quick mind. "Did people leave the village then?" she asked.

"Some did," Ramdas nodded. "But many stayed, rooted in love for this land. They shared what little they had, supported each other, and held fast to hope."

The circle grew quiet as the children imagined a world so different from their own—where survival depended not on technology, but on community and resilience.

Outside, beneath the spreading banyan tree, a group of villagers gathered. Their conversation was hushed but intense. Bhavna, the shopkeeper with a sharp gaze and even sharper tongue, voiced the fears many held but dared not say aloud.

"Progress is a double-edged sword," she said. "We want better schools and jobs for our children, yes. But at what cost? Will we lose our traditions, our way of life?"

Ramesh, the young father who had argued passionately for education, replied softly, "We must adapt, Bhavna. The world is changing beyond these hills. If we don't prepare our children, they will be lost."

Their debate echoed the larger struggle within the village—a tug-of-war between holding on and letting go.

Back in the classroom, Anika watched as the children shared their own family stories—tales of harvest festivals, ancient rituals, and the wisdom passed down through generations. The circle became a sanctuary where past and present intertwined, and the seeds of respect and understanding were sown.

But change was not always welcomed with open arms. One evening, as twilight painted the sky with purples and golds, Raghav received a message that stirred unrest. It came from Joshi, the distant official overseeing the school's funding, who insisted on immediate results and strict adherence to rigid metrics. His words carried an urgency that clashed with the village's measured pace.

Raghav sighed as he reread the letter. "Numbers and reports," he muttered. "They don't see the stories. They don't hear the laughter."

Anika placed a hand on his shoulder. "We must find a way to speak their language without losing ours."

The days that followed were filled with meetings, plans, and difficult conversations. Some villagers rallied behind Raghav's vision, while others retreated into suspicion. The cracks of division deepened.

One night, a heated village gathering erupted beneath the stars. Voices raised in fear, frustration, and passion. Accusations flew like sparks. Raghav stepped into the center, raising his hands for silence.

"We cannot move forward if we fight amongst ourselves," he said firmly. "Our strength is in unity, in honoring our past while building our future."

Slowly, the noise faded. Some nodded; others remained silent but thoughtful.

In the days that followed, small acts of reconciliation blossomed. Mannu organized a community garden where elders and children worked side by side, planting vegetables alongside memories. Under Anika's guidance, storytelling sessions rekindled respect for heritage and fostered new connections.

Raghav found solace beneath the banyan tree, feeling the pulse of generations beneath its roots. "We are not alone," he whispered to the night. "The past walks with us, guiding each step."

With renewed resolve, the village school became more than a place of learning—it became the heart of transformation. Children grew not only in knowledge but in empathy, courage, and belonging.

And as the sun rose each day over the hills, it illuminated a village standing at the cusp of change—its future shaped by the echoes of yesterday and the dreams of tomorrow.

Chapter 19:
Winds of Change

The dawn crept slowly over the village, bathing the hills in a gentle amber glow. The soft rustling of leaves whispered secrets of the night past, but the air was thick with anticipation — a feeling that something profound was about to unfold.

Raghav stood outside the modest schoolhouse, watching the first students arrive. Their faces were a mosaic of excitement, nervousness, and hope. Among them was Meera, clutching her worn notebook tightly, eyes shining with unspoken dreams. Today, unlike before, there was a subtle shift — an electric energy that seemed to hum beneath the ordinary.

Inside the classroom, Anika arranged her materials carefully. The walls, once bare, now brimmed with colorful posters depicting stories of inventors, poets, and revolutionaries — people who had changed the world through courage and conviction. It was more than a classroom; it was a sanctuary where possibilities blossomed.

As the children settled, Raghav's phone buzzed sharply. A message from the district education officer blinked on the screen, demanding an immediate report on test scores — a cold reminder of the bureaucratic pressures looming over their progress. Raghav swallowed the frustration, aware that behind these demands lay a system blind to the village's unique challenges and spirit.

The lesson began with a story — not one from a textbook, but a tale passed down from Ramdas, the village elder, about a young woman who had defied conventions to pursue education. Her name was Lakshmi, a name that had echoed through generations as a symbol of resilience.

"Lakshmi's story teaches us that the greatest battles are often within ourselves," Ramdas said, his voice steady and warm. "She faced doubt, fear, and opposition. Yet, she held on to her dreams."

Meera's hand shot up. "Did she ever think of giving up?"

Ramdas smiled gently. "Every day. But she chose to stand tall, even when the path was steep and lonely."

The children listened intently, their imaginations painting vivid pictures of Lakshmi's struggles and triumphs. For many, it was the first time history felt alive — not just facts to memorize, but human stories that resonated deeply.

Outside, the village was stirring with preparations for the upcoming harvest festival — a celebration that had long been a symbol of unity and renewal. But this year, the festival carried a new meaning, a chance to showcase the school's progress and rally the community behind a shared vision.

Raghav and Anika met with the festival committee, discussing plans to incorporate student performances and exhibitions that highlighted their learning journey. There was excitement, but also undercurrents of doubt from some elders wary of change.

Bhavna, ever vocal, voiced concerns at the meeting. "We must not lose who we are in this rush for progress. The festival is our tradition, not a stage for politics."

Raghav nodded thoughtfully. "Traditions are the roots that hold us firm. But the branches must grow to reach the sun."

The festival preparations breathed new life into the village. Children practiced songs and dances, rehearsed speeches, and created artwork reflecting their hopes. The community garden flourished, a testament to collective effort and shared dreams.

Yet, beneath the surface, challenges persisted. The education officer's reports loomed, and whispers of budget cuts spread uneasily. Raghav found himself at crossroads — balancing administrative demands with the fragile heartbeat of a village yearning for transformation.

One evening, as twilight softened the sky, Raghav sat with Anika beneath the banyan tree, sharing worries and hopes.

"Do you think we're making a difference?" he asked, voice tinged with doubt.

Anika looked up at the stars just beginning to twinkle. "Change is slow, Raghav. But every seed we plant now will one day become a mighty tree."

Their conversation was interrupted by the arrival of Ramdas, who carried a bundle of old photographs — sepia-toned memories of the village decades past.

"Look," he said, spreading the pictures gently. "These are reminders of where we've been. And why we must keep moving forward."

As the harvest festival dawned, the village was alive with colors, music, and laughter. The school's pavilion stood proudly at the center, adorned with student projects and stories. Parents, elders, and visitors gathered, witnessing the blossoming of young minds and the rekindling of community spirit.

Lakshmi's story was told anew, through drama and song, inspiring tears and applause. Meera took the stage, her voice steady as she shared her own dreams — dreams once whispered only to herself.

Raghav watched from the crowd, heart swelling with pride and hope. The winds of change were not just blowing; they were carrying a promise — that from the echoes of yesterday, a brighter tomorrow could rise.

Chapter 20:
The Fire Beneath the Ashes

The rain came suddenly.

It started as a whisper—soft droplets tapping on the dusty rooftops—then grew into a drumming roar that soaked the village in a matter of minutes. The earth sighed in relief as the parched soil drank greedily, releasing a scent that only those who've known drought understand—a rich, earthy perfume of rebirth. For the villagers of Dharigunj, the rain meant something more than a shift in weather. It was an omen. A cleansing. A reminder that life could change in an instant.

Raghav stood in the doorway of the school, watching the downpour with furrowed brows. The festival had passed, leaving behind echoes of song, flashes of color, and the quiet awe of those who had witnessed transformation—especially the elders, many of whom had been skeptical until they saw their grandchildren reciting poetry or acting out historical revolutions with passion that burned brighter than any textbook could contain.

But despite the celebration's success, a storm brewed beyond the clouds—a bureaucratic one.

Earlier that morning, a letter had arrived from the district office. Not just a routine report request. This one carried an ultimatum: standardize or be defunded.

"Your institution must align with the state-mandated academic structure by the next quarter. Failure to do so will result in the revocation of grants and withdrawal of district-supported programs."

Raghav's fingers trembled as he folded the letter, slipping it into the bottom drawer of his desk. He didn't tell Anika right away. He needed to think.

Was it possible to keep the soul of their teaching while conforming to an outdated system that measured success only in numbers and rote facts?

That evening, as the rain softened to a drizzle, Anika found him still in the classroom, the oil lamp flickering shadows across his tired face.

"You're hiding something," she said, not unkindly.

Raghav handed her the letter without a word. She read it slowly, lips tightening.

"They don't understand," she whispered. "They never have."

"We've shown them results," he said. "But it's never enough. It's like trying to measure the warmth of a sunrise with a thermometer."

Anika looked at the children's drawings pinned to the wall—Meera's depiction of the Banyan tree, Aarav's poem about his grandfather's journey from a plow to a printing press, Tara's watercolor of a classroom under the stars.

"They're not just learning facts here, Raghav," she said. "They're learning to live."

But it wasn't just the district looming large. The undercurrent of unrest in the village had grown louder. Some elders, emboldened by whispers from outside towns, began warning that too much change would erode the village's essence. That the school was no longer just a place of learning—but a factory for rebellion.

In one such meeting, held under the ancient neem tree near the well, Bhavna stood once more to speak.

"They now teach our children to question. To dream beyond the fields. Is that what we want?" she asked.

A silence fell.

Then, Ramdas rose—slower than he once did, but his voice carried the weight of generations.

"We once believed the earth was flat, Bhavna. Until someone dared to ask a question."

The crowd murmured. Some nodded. Others walked away, uncomfortable.

That night, Meera sat by her window, watching lightning fork across the sky. Her mother was sewing by lantern light, quiet. Meera's father, who once doubted the school's value, now listened to her read poems aloud. She had changed, and so had they. But she had overheard the whispers—the school might close. That the government wanted something else. Her heart tightened.

The next morning, the children found a notice pinned to the school gate:

"Classes suspended until further directive from district authorities."

Confusion reigned.

Aarav stared at the paper, eyes wide. "What does this mean?"

"It means," Raghav said, stepping out with heavy shoulders, "we need to find another way."

But where there is fire, there is also fuel.

The villagers gathered that evening—every mother, every grandfather, every child who had once trembled before a blackboard but now stood tall with knowledge in their hands.

"We won't wait for permission to educate our children," Anika declared, her voice ringing in the rain-slicked courtyard. "If they shut the doors, we'll open the windows. If they take the roof, we'll teach under trees."

It was Meera who stepped forward next.

"I can teach the younger ones," she said, holding her notebooks like a sword. "Just like you taught me."

Something shifted in that moment. The school had not been the building. It had been the people. The spark caught fire.

Classes resumed—in homes, in courtyards, beneath the banyan tree. Raghav split his time between subjects and strategy, while Anika drafted a new curriculum that honored state requirements but kept the soul of their methods intact.

Ramdas began mentoring older students in village history and traditional wisdom. Tara's father volunteered to teach carpentry in the afternoons. Even Bhavna, moved by the children's refusal to stop learning, began preparing midday meals for the impromptu classrooms.

And when the district officer arrived two weeks later, expecting silence, he found song.

Children reciting lessons in unison from the temple steps. Teenagers discussing physics under tarpaulins. Parents reading aloud with their children in village squares.

"You've disobeyed a direct order," the officer said, sternly facing Raghav.

"No," Raghav replied. "We followed a higher one—the duty to learn, to grow, and to serve our community."

The officer paused. Then he said, "You've made my job harder. But... I see something rare here."

He left without revoking their funds. Without threatening again. Something had changed. Perhaps even in him.

As the weeks passed, the school was formally reopened. But it was no longer the same school. It had become a movement. A symbol. A living, breathing proof that transformation does not wait for approval.

And in the quiet of that renewed dawn, as children returned to their rebuilt desks, as parents smiled with pride, as Meera taught the younger students how to hold a pencil and chase a question, Raghav looked toward the horizon.

The fire beneath the ashes had not destroyed them. It had forged something indestructible.

A future that no storm, no system, no silence could ever erase.

Chapter 21:
The Light We Carry

The sun had not yet risen when Raghav woke, but he knew this would be the day everything changed.

The monsoon clouds had retreated into distant silence. The air was heavy with the scent of soaked earth and something else — a quiet finality, as if the village itself was holding its breath. Yet there was no dread in his heart. Only resolve.

He looked at the small school building — repaired, reshaped, reborn. The whitewashed walls carried more than paint; they held the voices of children, the dreams whispered under lantern light, the hope that had once flickered and now blazed with undeniable strength.

Anika met him by the gate, shawl pulled tightly around her shoulders. Her eyes met his, unreadable for a moment. Then she smiled.

"They're ready," she said.

The final community meeting was scheduled at dawn. Not just a review of the school, or an address from officials — but a gathering to decide what Dharigunj would become next.

Would they return to the way things were? Or step fully into the light they had all helped ignite?

Ramdas had requested to speak first. The villagers gathered in the courtyard — children in uniforms stitched at home, mothers clutching notebooks alongside their little ones, fathers standing taller than they ever had before.

The old man, whose hands had once tilled the same soil as his ancestors, now stood with his walking stick like a staff of wisdom.

"I was wrong," he said without hesitation. "I once believed tradition was stone — fixed, immovable. But tradition is not what we protect from change. It's what we pass through it."

A hush swept the crowd.

"You all saw what happened when the rains came. Not just water, but new life. These children — they are our monsoon. Our renewal. We cannot go back."

Raghav stepped forward next, his voice soft, but steady.

"We built this place on questions," he said. "What if learning wasn't a burden, but a birthright? What if a girl could teach her brother? What if a classroom had no walls?"

He paused, letting the questions linger.

"And now we must ask another: What if we trusted ourselves to lead this future — not because someone gave us permission, but because we finally believe we can?"

There was silence. Then, from the back, Meera's voice rose: "We don't want to be told who we are. We want to discover it ourselves."

Applause broke — not the polite kind, but the kind that surged from chests like thunder. A ripple of agreement, not just with words, but with conviction.

For the first time in generations, the village of Dharigunj voted unanimously — not for leaders, but for a vision. A school that belonged not to the state, not to a syllabus, but to its people.

That afternoon, something extraordinary happened.

A letter arrived — not from the district, but the capital.

The Ministry of Education had heard about Dharigunj's revolution. A delegation would arrive in a week. The village would be studied. A model for decentralized, human-centered education might be born — if the people agreed to share what they had built.

Anika stared at the letter, then looked at Raghav.

"They want to learn from us?"

He nodded slowly. "Yes. Because we stopped asking for validation. And started teaching from truth."

That evening, the village celebrated not with fireworks, but with stories.

Each child recited a poem they had written. Mothers shared what they had learned from their children. Ramdas told tales of his youth, not to warn, but to encourage.

And Meera, standing under the banyan tree, read her final lines:

"They asked us what we carried. We said: the weight of forgotten dreams. They asked us what we found. We said: a light we didn't know we had."

As night settled, the stars emerged — one by one, quiet witnesses to the promise fulfilled. No one spoke of endings. Only beginnings.

The school had been saved. But more importantly, it had been reclaimed — not as a building, but as a beacon.

The journey that had started with a single frustrated man in a crumbling classroom had become a wildfire of awakening.

Dharigunj was no longer just a village. It was a vision. A living, breathing proof that when people rise together, not even the oldest shadows can stay.

And as the first light of the next dawn crept over the rooftops, a new chapter — unwritten, unknown, but entirely theirs — had already begun.

Chapter 22:
The Turning Point

The café was packed. Not in the comfortable, laughter-laced way of university hangouts or startup meetups. This felt more like a chamber of trial — young voices buzzing like electric wires, tables cluttered with coffee rings and notebooks, and eyes flicking toward the projector screen with a hunger that was far more than curiosity.

Raghav stood at the back, half-hidden behind a pillar smeared with chalk quotes from tech philosophers and long-dead poets. The air inside was damp with monsoon humidity, and every ceiling fan above spun with a limp determination. Beside him, Anika shifted from one foot to the other, biting her lip the way she always did when she felt a storm brewing but couldn't tell whether it was internal or coming from outside.

On the screen, a girl appeared — maybe seven years old, her hair in two tight braids, her uniform faded at the collar. She sat on a straw mat in a one-room village school with cracked walls and crooked windows. But the moment she touched the screen of the EduInnovate tablet, the room stilled. The child's voice, unsure but brave, read out the English sentence onscreen. It wasn't flawless. She paused in the middle. But she finished it — all by herself.

The applause in the café was spontaneous, loud, and unfamiliar to Raghav's ears. It was the applause of recognition, the kind he had never received in his village, not when he won the science fair, not when he left for Mumbai, not even when he returned with better shoes and softer speech. Here, people were clapping not for him — but for an idea he had once whispered into code at 3 a.m. under the dim light of a dying lamp.

On the café walls, projectors replayed the now-viral clip. A watermark in the corner read: *The Story of the Silent Builder: Raghav Mishra's Village Vision.* A media outlet had picked it up two days ago. Twenty-four hours later, it had crossed a million views. Now, strangers knew his face. People tagged him on LinkedIn, quoted him on Twitter, messaged him promises, advice, and threats on Instagram.

He hadn't responded to a single one.

After the video ended, the crowd dissolved into small clusters of conversation. Raghav stepped out without saying goodbye to anyone. Not out of arrogance — he just didn't know how to explain the knot in his throat.

The taxi ride to the investor meeting was quiet. Anika sat beside him, typing notes into her phone. Outside, Mumbai stretched like a restless dream — its billboards taller than its people, its streets slick with rain, its voices shouting over one another in an orchestra of survival.

The building they entered was glass and steel and perfect symmetry. It towered above the slums they'd passed just minutes ago. At the top floor, past fingerprint scanners and a polished receptionist who smiled like a vending machine, they entered a conference room that smelled faintly of cold coffee and ambition.

Three men waited inside. Two leaned back with the confidence of people used to being obeyed. The third, younger, sharp-suited, with a watch that could buy a house in Chandanpur, stood as they entered.

"Raghav," he said with a disarming grin. "Ishaan Mehta. Welcome."

They shook hands. Ishaan's grip was firm — but not the kind that offered support. It was the kind that measured the strength of your bones.

The meeting began with compliments.

"I saw your video. Beautiful storytelling. That's what this space has been missing — heart."

Raghav forced a smile, nodding politely. He recognized the dance — praise before proposition, warmth before transaction.

Ishaan clicked his tablet. The lights dimmed slightly. A new pitch deck blinked onto the screen. Not the one Priya had prepared.

"We did some brand brainstorming," Ishaan said. "Just a mock-up. Same core — new name, new look, new strategy."

The new name was *EduSpark*.

The new logo looked sleek, corporate. Polished.

Gone was the small trishul watermark Anika had designed — the tribute to Raghav's grandfather.

Raghav's pulse slowed. Not in calm — in calculation. He let Ishaan continue, words swimming past like oil on water.

"We focus on urban slums now. Kids with smartphones but no guidance. We streamline the app — one language, English. We lock premium features. Introduce ads. Get user data. Build fast. Exit faster."

Anika stiffened beside him. Her silence was a warning bell.

Ishaan leaned back, lacing his fingers together. "Raghav, let me be honest. You've built a dream. But dreams need money to walk."

Raghav spoke quietly. "And you want to buy the legs."

Ishaan didn't flinch. "We want to put those legs in running shoes."

There was a pause. Heavy. Pregnant with consequences.

Anika cleared her throat. "What about the children who don't speak English? The teachers who helped us build content? The villages who trusted us?"

Ishaan turned to her, his smile still fixed. "They'll adapt. Or they'll be left behind. That's the nature of growth."

Something broke in Raghav then. Not his temper. Not his faith. But the leash of hesitation.

He stood up.

"We didn't build this to be scalable. We built it to be seen. To be heard. To give a voice to places where even the internet was a rumor."

Ishaan nodded, slow and detached. "And that voice is now valuable. Let us amplify it. Clean it. Monetize it."

Raghav's voice turned steel. "No."

Ishaan blinked. Just once.

"You'll walk away from seven crores in the first round?"

"I'll walk away from anything that demands I erase the reason I started."

There was a beat of silence. Then Ishaan shrugged, almost amused. "You'll learn. All revolutionaries do. Eventually."

Outside, the rain had stopped. But the clouds hadn't left.

Back at the office, Priya exploded.

"You said no?! Without consulting the team?"

"I listened," Raghav replied. "And I chose."

"We could've scaled! We could've paid everyone full-time. We could've—"

"—become what we swore we wouldn't," he finished.

Anika said nothing. But when she passed him a cup of lukewarm tea, he saw it in her eyes: not agreement, not relief — but the deep, silent kind of loyalty that doesn't need words.

That night, he sat alone at his desk, staring at the screen.

His inbox blinked with unread messages. His phone buzzed with investor follow-ups.

He ignored them all.

Instead, he opened the dashboard.

Four hundred and seventy-three new downloads. Eighty-seven new feedback notes from teachers in remote districts. Twelve new story uploads in Bhojpuri.

Real. Quiet. Steady.

He opened his email. Wrote the response to Ishaan. No theatrics. No bitterness.

Just truth.

He signed his name and hovered his finger over *Send*.

Outside, the city roared with traffic, celebration, collapse.

Inside the office, a silence stood tall.

He clicked.

And with that one decision, everything that followed would become a consequence.

Not of mistake.

But of courage.

Chapter 23:
Fractures and Fault Lines

It began with silence.

Not the comforting kind that follows a day well-spent, but the heavy, reluctant kind that creeps into a room after something irreversible has happened. The office that had once buzzed with scattered conversations, late-night laughter, and the soothing hum of shared purpose now felt like a cracked monument—still standing, but under strain no one dared speak aloud.

Raghav sat at the far end of the table, laptop closed, hands clenched together like he was trying to hold something broken from falling apart. Across from him, Priya flipped through the latest operational report with such sharpness in her eyes it could've cut paper without touching it.

"You should have discussed it with us," she said without looking up. Her voice was calm, calculated, but laced with a heat that threatened to ignite if struck wrong.

"I did," Raghav replied.

"No, you *told* us. There's a difference."

Anika stood by the window, arms crossed, watching the rain drip down the glass in slow, streaking lines. The city outside continued its chaotic symphony — cars honking, vendors shouting, thunder grumbling in the distance — but inside, time had shrunk to the space between accusations.

"We're not children, Raghav," Priya continued. "We've sacrificed just as much as you. We've earned a vote."

"You want democracy," he said softly, "but you weren't in that room. You didn't see what they wanted to do to this."

Priya slammed the report down. "Seven crores. That money could've changed everything. Salaries. Infrastructure. Expansion. Stability. You threw it away for... ideals."

That word stung more than it should have — *ideals*. As if belief was some naive luxury.

"Ideals built this," Raghav said, his voice dangerously quiet. "Not capital. Not contacts. We didn't start this to sell it the moment someone waved a cheque."

"No," Priya said coldly, "you started this because you were angry. Angry at a system that forgot you. But you forgot something too — anger doesn't scale. Vision does."

The room fell into stillness, not from agreement but exhaustion. Words had become weapons, and none of them wanted to draw more blood.

Anika finally turned. "We need a break. All of us."

But there was no time for breaks.

The next morning, they arrived to find the power out. A fuse had blown overnight, frying three old desktop machines used by the content translation team. Their last backup was two weeks old. An intern had unplugged the surge protector to charge his phone. A simple mistake. A devastating cost.

The loss was more than data — it was time, trust, and momentum.

The incident cracked open something that had long been forming in the shadows — doubt.

The kind that didn't shout, but whispered.

What if we're not ready?
What if he's not capable?
What if we're wrong?

Tensions spilled over. Meetings turned into debates. Tasks went undone. Messages unanswered. Emails ignored. The app's user feedback dropped by fourteen percent. A district coordinator resigned over stress. Field visits were delayed. Teachers stopped reporting bugs.

The cracks weren't just operational.

They were emotional.

One evening, Raghav walked into the office late to find a message scribbled on the whiteboard in red marker:

"Purpose is not immunity from chaos."

No one admitted to writing it.

But everyone understood it.

Three days later, the storm broke.

It was a Friday evening when Priya called for an emergency meeting. Everyone came, but not everyone sat down. The air was thick with resignation.

"I'm stepping away," she said. "For now."

Raghav's breath caught in his throat.

"What do you mean 'stepping away'?" Anika asked slowly.

"I mean I need distance. This place... this version of us... it's not what I signed up for. And if I stay, I'll only grow bitter."

No one interrupted. Priya was the spine of operations, the keeper of spreadsheets, deadlines, donor reports, and budget estimates. Losing her was like losing gravity.

"Is it because of me?" Raghav asked.

Priya turned to him. Her eyes weren't angry anymore. Just tired. "It's because of all of us. And none of us. It's because I don't recognize what we've become."

She left without packing. Just her notebook, phone, and the pen Anika had gifted her on their first donor win. The door closed softly behind her. It sounded louder than a scream.

For the next few days, the office functioned like a wounded animal — limping, twitching, silent in strange places.

Anika tried to hold things together, stepping into Priya's role while keeping her own. Her mornings began at six and ended past midnight. Raghav tried to help, but his words landed flat. Every suggestion felt like a command. Every apology, a delay. He could feel her slipping into a kind of solitude that looked like strength but was slowly draining her from the inside out.

He wanted to say so many things.

But all he managed one night, under the buzzing tube light, was, "I'm sorry."

Anika nodded, not looking at him. "We'll be okay. We have to be."

But her voice was thin. Brittle.

Like hope written in pencil.

The next fracture came not from within — but from outside.

A leaked screenshot of their internal user data dashboard made its way onto a startup gossip forum. Someone had posted it anonymously, with the caption:

"Rural edtech startup fakes growth metrics? Users inflated?"

The post exploded. Comment sections filled with doubt. DMs from donors trickled in with polite urgency. Even the foundation that had awarded them the initial seed grant requested a formal clarification.

They weren't guilty. But they were now forced to prove their innocence in a world that didn't wait.

Raghav spent forty-eight hours with no sleep, digging through logs, checking access points, tracking timestamps. The leaker had used a shared device. No trail. No confession.

It didn't matter. Perception was reality.

The narrative had turned.

Late one night, after a particularly brutal call with the foundation's legal consultant, Raghav stood alone in the kitchen, staring into the electric kettle as it boiled.

He didn't hear Anika enter.

"You haven't eaten," she said gently.

He shook his head.

"I think I lost them," he murmured. "All of them. You. Priya. The team. Maybe even myself."

Anika stepped beside him. She didn't speak for a long time. Just stood there, shoulder to shoulder.

Then she whispered, "You didn't lose us. You forgot to *lead* us."

Raghav turned. Her eyes weren't accusing. Just honest.

"We followed you because we believed in what you believed," she continued. "Not because you were always right. But because you were always *true*."

"Ishaan was right," Raghav said. "I don't know how to scale. I only know how to start."

"Then let's start again," she said.

And in that moment — exhausted, heartbroken, unsure — they didn't plan a new pitch or strategy.

They just stood in a room filled with ghosts of choices, and promised not to let the cracks become collapse.

Not yet.

Chapter 24:
Whispers from Home

The bus to Chandanpur was three hours late, and not a single person seemed surprised.

Raghav sat on a wooden bench at the station, one leg tapping uncontrollably, a duffel bag at his feet and silence pressed against his ribs. The din around him was familiar: porters shouting, chaiwalas weaving through crowds with aluminum kettles, babies crying, vendors repeating the same phrases with a rhythm born of exhaustion. It should've comforted him.

It didn't.

He wasn't here for comfort.

He had returned to remember who he was—because somewhere in the storm of broken trust, lost teammates, and headlines that questioned his integrity, something had slipped out of him without saying goodbye.

The journey home passed in patches. Rice fields blurred into forest, then into cracked highways and mustard-yellow billboards. The bus wheezed like an old man climbing a hill he didn't want to conquer. No one made eye contact. That, at least, had not changed.

When Raghav finally stepped off at the dusty crossroad two kilometers from his village, the sun was sinking behind the palms, staining the sky with red and rust. A farmer passed with a wooden plough balanced on one shoulder and stared at him like he was a memory that didn't fit anymore.

His house appeared slowly through the dusk, its walls just as faded, its windows still covered in the same floral cloth curtains his mother had stitched when he was twelve. A lone goat stood tied to the neem tree. A bicycle leaned against the back wall, half-covered in mud. Time had not waited here. But neither had it moved fast enough to forget.

He didn't knock. He didn't need to.

The door creaked open, and his mother's eyes widened—not with surprise, but with something deeper, something heavier than joy.

She didn't say a word. Just walked forward and placed a trembling palm on his cheek, as if checking whether he was real.

His father stood in the corner, arms folded, face unreadable.

"You came," he said simply.

"I had to," Raghav replied.

Dinner was quiet.

A steel plate. Rice and potatoes. The smell of ghee that tugged at old hunger.

His mother asked about the trains. The weather. The food in Mumbai. But not about the company. Not about the article. Not about the decision that had derailed everything.

His father only spoke once.

"You're tired."

It wasn't a question.

Raghav nodded.

"Then stay. Just for a few days. Let the dust settle."

Outside, crickets began their nightly orchestra. Inside, the clock ticked a little too loudly.

The next morning, he walked the length of the village alone.

Past the banyan tree where he had first drawn circuits in the dirt with a stick.

Past the school whose broken benches had shaped his spine.

Past the stream where he once whispered code to the wind, not to be understood, but to feel less alone.

Everything looked smaller. Not because it had shrunk, but because he had grown taller in different directions.

Still, the whispers found him.

"Did you hear? He turned down crores."

"He was in the newspaper. Maybe the papers lie."

"They say the app's failing. But who knows."

He smiled at no one. Nodded at everyone.

At noon, he visited the school.

The same blackboard. The same smell of chalk and iron windows. But there was something new now — a stack of tablets in the corner, neatly shelved, charging from a solar panel bolted onto the outer wall.

The teacher, a young woman named Reena, recognized him instantly.

"You're him," she said with a shy smile. "We use your app every Thursday."

Raghav laughed softly. "Only Thursday?"

"Sometimes Friday too. If the kids ask nicely."

He watched as children huddled around a device, tracing words in their own language, their fingers hesitant but hopeful.

He didn't say much. Just watched.

And in that watching, something stirred.

Not pride.

Not nostalgia.

Something simpler.

Something like belonging.

That night, he sat with his mother in the courtyard under the stars.

She ground spices in a stone bowl, and the air smelled of rain and chillies.

"I saw your face in a paper once," she said. "It was folded near the pickle jar. You looked tired."

"I was," Raghav said.

"Still are."

She paused. Then added, "You don't have to carry everything, beta. Even the river has a bed beneath it."

He didn't reply. Just leaned his head against her shoulder like he used to when storms outside made him flinch.

"Do you think I was wrong?" he asked quietly. "To walk away from all that money?"

She didn't answer immediately. The pestle slowed in her hand.

"I think," she said finally, "if it cost you your peace, it was never wealth."

The words settled into his bones like warmth.

He didn't sleep that night. He sat under the neem tree until morning, notebook in hand, rewriting lines of code that weren't technical. They were philosophical. Ethical. Foundational.

On the fourth day, he left.

At the bus stop, his father handed him a cloth pouch tied with a rubber band. Inside was the old silver trishul pendant — polished now, the chain repaired.

"This was your grandfather's. He fought wars you'll never hear about. Not with swords. With choices."

Raghav closed his fingers around it.

When the bus pulled in, he climbed aboard and turned to look back.

Not at the house. But at the fields behind it.

The places that had shaped him without asking for credit.

Back in Mumbai, the office smelled of stale coffee and something else — anticipation.

Anika sat at her desk, sorting documents. She looked up as he entered and didn't smile.

"You okay?" she asked.

"No," he said. "But I'm ready."

She nodded. "Then let's rebuild."

He placed the pouch on the table between them.

"We don't scale for growth," he said. "We scale for reach. No branding. No dilution. We go deeper before we go wide."

Her eyes flicked to the pendant. Then to him.

"Then we begin again."

He nodded.

But not with a smile.

With a vow.

Chapter 25: The Pivot

The office was quiet when Raghav returned—not dead, but still. Like a forest after a storm, waiting to see what had survived. Some desks were empty. Some chairs never pushed back. On the whiteboard, old plans stared at him like abandoned blueprints from a civilization that had lost faith in its architects.

He stood in the center of the room, eyes closed, palms open.

He wasn't looking for answers.

He was listening for the faint heartbeat of a dream he'd once promised to protect.

Behind him, a door creaked.

Anika entered, face drawn but eyes steady. She didn't ask him where he'd been. She didn't need to.

He looked at her, then at the handful of staff still loyal enough to show up.

"Let's not rebuild what broke," he said softly. "Let's build something new."

The pivot wasn't born from ambition. It was born from failure.

For weeks, the team had tried to pretend things could go back to normal. That with a few tweaks, a couple of emails, and a new funding proposal, they could plug the holes in the sinking ship.

But the truth was this: EduInnovate, in its original form, was not enough.

Not enough for the children who needed more than alphabets.

Not enough for the teachers who wanted more than tools.

Not enough for the villages that didn't just want access — they wanted agency.

And not enough for Raghav, who had realized that delivering education was only part of the battle.

What came after learning?

What happened to the child who could read — but had no job?

What happened to the girl who mastered language — but was still married off before sixteen?

Knowledge without power was a candle in a cave.

So, he pivoted.

Not to scale wide.

To scale *deep*.

EduInnovate 2.0 would not just teach.

It would empower.

The first idea was messy, half-baked, and dismissed by almost everyone: a decentralized model of community-powered learning hubs — but fused with **local content creation and micro-skilling.**

They would not just feed children data.

They would teach them how to generate, interpret, and **own** it.

Every student would become a creator. Every teacher, a community leader. Every village, a node in a growing network of knowledge ecosystems.

Skeptics rolled their eyes.

"Sounds like a utopia," one of the mentors texted. "Sounds expensive."

Raghav replied with a single line: *Utopia is what the world calls a village that dares to dream.*

He never got a reply

The pilot began in Bhagalpur.

A district known for its handloom, its heat, and its quiet resilience.

Anika led the operations. Raghav stayed behind, coordinating tech.

They didn't talk much anymore. Not because of anger — but because both of them were learning a new language: the language of starting over.

In Bhagalpur, the learning hubs were small — sometimes just a tiled room in the back of a temple or a cow shed swept clean. But they came alive in the evenings. Children gathered around donated screens. Volunteers read aloud from new modules. Grandmothers listened in the corner, pretending not to cry when they understood words they'd never been taught.

The innovation was not in the interface.

It was in what they allowed.

Kids began submitting their own stories — in Bhojpuri, in Maithili, in Magahi.

Tailors uploaded how-to videos in Hindi on sewing blouse patterns.

One old man, a potter named Rajnath, taught kids ratios and fractions using clay.

For the first time, EduInnovate was not just teaching.

It was *learning back*.

One evening, as Anika wrapped up a session in a makeshift hub, a girl named Kanchan approached her.

She was twelve. Thin. Bright eyes. Callused hands.

"I made something," Kanchan said, shyly holding up a piece of folded paper.

It was a comic strip — drawn in pencil, rough and shaky, but bursting with imagination.

A girl with a slingshot fought a monster made of ignorance. Her weapon? Words. Sentences. Questions.

"I want to put her in the app," Kanchan whispered. "So other girls can see she's not afraid."

Anika didn't speak.

She just hugged her.

And knew in that moment — the pivot was real.

Back in Mumbai, Raghav worked like a man possessed.

He redesigned the app architecture to accommodate creator uploads.

He rewrote the permissions engine to prioritize safety and transparency.

He turned EduInnovate into a platform — not a product.

But the tech was only half the battle.

Funding was still short.

Servers were running on borrowed cloud credits.

Field trainers were volunteers.

But what they lacked in money, they made up for in momentum.

One night, Anika returned from Bhagalpur with two new teachers and a bag full of locally written storybooks. She dropped them on Raghav's desk.

"We need to digitize these," she said.

He looked up. "All of them?"

"Every last page."

He opened the first one.

On the inside cover was a dedication: *To the daughter I wasn't allowed to name.*

He didn't sleep that night.

He scanned and uploaded all ten books.

At dawn, he added a new category to the app:

"Stories from Home."

By noon, it had 2,300 views.

By the end of the week, it had 12,000.

The algorithm had nothing to do with it.

These stories *belonged* to the children. So they stayed. They returned. They shared.

Then came the letter.

A simple brown envelope addressed to "The Founder, EduInnovate."

Inside was a note scribbled in blue ink:

Sir, I am writing this myself. Not my father. Not my teacher. Me.

I used to think learning was only for people in cities. Now I know learning can come from people like us too.

One day, I will write a book. You will see.

– Reema Devi, Class 6

The letter sat on Raghav's desk for three days.

He didn't move it.

He couldn't.

Every time he saw it, he felt something inside him realign — not like a gear clicking into place, but like a wound beginning to close.

By the end of the quarter, EduInnovate had created over 500 pieces of local content from ten districts.

Student retention doubled.

Three NGOs signed on as partners.

And one state education board requested a presentation.

Raghav declined the speaking engagement.

Instead, he sent them the voice recording of Kanchan's comic story — her narrating her warrior girl's journey with pride and unfiltered courage.

He didn't need applause.

He needed them to listen.

And when they did — really did — they didn't ask him to change the model.

They asked him how fast he could bring it to twenty districts.

On a Sunday night, as the rains returned to Mumbai, Raghav stood again on the rooftop of the hostel.

Anika joined him, two mugs of tea in hand.

They watched lightning split the sky over the ocean.

"I never thought the pivot would come from failure," he said.

"It didn't," she replied. "It came from truth."

He turned to her. "Do you think we'll make it?"

She shrugged.

"Maybe. Maybe not. But if we fall now... at least we fall forward."

They didn't toast.

They just stood there.

Two warriors.

Two believers.

Watching the storm, not with fear —

But with the quiet thrill of those who know they've chosen the harder path...

And are no longer afraid to walk it.

Chapter 26:
The Spark of Scale

It started with a letterhead. Plain. Stamped. Official.

Subject: *Proposal for Partnership Pilot under Rural Digital Literacy Expansion Scheme.*

Sender: Department of Education, Government of Bihar.

The ink was still drying when Anika brought it to Raghav's desk. She placed the envelope down like it held explosives. In a way, it did.

He read the document twice. Then a third time. His hands did not tremble. But his thoughts did.

The government had taken notice.

Not of them as a startup. But as a solution.

The proposal was direct: Implement EduInnovate's new community-led content platform across 100 blocks in rural Bihar. Train government teachers. Integrate vernacular content. Track metrics. Report outcomes.

If successful, the program would go statewide.

Raghav stared at the signature at the bottom—an IAS officer named Meenal Rao. He'd never met her, but she'd watched Kanchan's comic strip video during a conference and apparently stayed up all night going through the Stories from Home archive.

They didn't need to apply.

They'd already been chosen.

For the first time, Raghav felt a fear he couldn't name.

Not of failure.

Of *scale*.

The first meeting with the officials happened on a humid Tuesday in Patna.

The conference room was clinical—white walls, chrome fans, filtered water in glass jugs. Meenal Rao arrived wearing a crisp khadi sari and a Bluetooth earpiece she never removed, even when it wasn't in use. Her handshake was firm, but not aggressive.

She didn't ask about revenue.

She didn't mention funding.

Her only question was, "How fast can you move?"

Raghav hesitated. "Fast enough to make it real. Slow enough to make it last."

She nodded. "Good answer. Bad business model."

Everyone laughed. Except Raghav.

This wasn't a joke to him.

Back in Mumbai, the office turned into a war room.

Maps covered the walls. District names were turned into code names—Banka became Falcon. Jamui was Jaguar. Kishanganj was K2.

Anika organized the strategy team.

Two new hires were made: one former NGO field officer named Zeeshan and a data analyst named Tara who only wore black and asked questions like a prosecutor.

Daily stand-ups turned into twice-daily.

Calls flooded in from village panchayats, eager to be included.

There was no going back.

The platform that had once been a whisper was now being handed a megaphone.

But growth did not come without blood.

Three weeks into rollout, a glitch brought everything crashing.

The offline sync feature, meant to auto-update the app in areas without 4G, failed during testing. Instead of syncing content, it corrupted half the new uploads. Hours of stories. Teacher modules. Child-created comics. Gone.

The team was devastated. One teacher from Araria cried on a Zoom call.

"I promised them their poems would be seen. They stayed after school for *this*."

Anika's face was pale. Tara didn't speak for an hour. Zeeshan blamed himself for not testing harder.

Raghav didn't yell. He didn't console.

He sat at his desk for seven straight hours, rewriting the patch line by line.

At 4:23 a.m., it worked.

The data returned.

Not all of it.

But enough.

Still, damage had been done.

WhatsApp groups with educators began to turn hostile.

"Do they think we're test dummies?"

"This is just another city idea dumped on us."

"They come, they break things, they leave."

Raghav knew those words.

He had once said them about others.

Now, they were being said about him.

For two days, he didn't speak to anyone.

He just listened. To criticism. To pain. To betrayal.

And then he acted.

They launched the **Sunlight Protocol**.

Named by a child from Samastipur who said, "If you want people to trust you, don't show them a torch—just pull the curtains."

The protocol included:

- Daily transparency logs made public.
- Every contributor shown exactly where their content went and who used it.
- A "Fix It" button on the app homepage allowing real-time bug reporting with video.
- Direct village-level ambassadors empowered to approve uploads.

They stopped being an app.

They became a movement.

Meenal Rao called Raghav ten days later.

"Smart recovery," she said.

"We got lucky," he replied.

"No," she said, "you got humble. That's rarer."

The partnership was greenlit.

One hundred blocks.

Four hundred schools.

Fifty thousand users.

Launch date: four weeks.

In the middle of the chaos, Anika's voice came through like the quietest drumbeat.

"You need to prepare."

"For what?" Raghav asked.

"For being seen."

She was right.

So far, EduInnovate had thrived in silence. Now the world wanted a face.

The media reached out. Forbes India. YourStory. NDTV.

Raghav said no to all of them.

Until one letter arrived. Handwritten.

From a 10-year-old named Danish.

Bhaiya, you are coming on TV, right? If not, how will my Dadi believe I helped make a story?

So Raghav said yes.

The segment was five minutes.

But it changed everything.

Footage of village kids reading their own tales, teachers sharing audio modules, and a slow zoom-in on Kanchan's drawing aired on prime time.

Raghav spoke little.

But he ended with this:

"We used to ask how to bring change to the village. Now, the village *teaches* us how to change."

Overnight, app installs doubled.

But so did expectations.

Requests came in from three other states.

Big education foundations knocked again.

Meenal Rao offered him a word of caution: "Do not let admiration become addiction."

He wrote it down and taped it to his desk.

The night before the statewide rollout, Raghav sat with Anika on the hostel rooftop again.

They didn't bring tea.

Just silence.

"Are you afraid?" she asked.

"No," he said. "I'm alert."

She smiled.

"Good," she said. "Because scale is not a ladder. It's a mirror."

Raghav looked up at the sky.

Somewhere far away, a girl was learning her first word.

Somewhere closer, a boy was recording his grandmother's lullaby.

And somewhere inside him, he felt it.

Not pride.

Not victory.

Something older.

Something like responsibility.

He whispered to the sky:

"Don't let this grow faster than I can love it."

Chapter 27:
Storms and Sacrifice

The storm didn't arrive with thunder.

It arrived quietly, on a sunlit morning, when the air was too still and the silence too wide. Raghav should've known then. After everything—the battles with doubt, the reckoning with truth, the pivot, the scale—he should have known that something was coming.

But success has a way of dimming your instincts. The moment you start to breathe again, the world reminds you that peace is not permanent. Not here. Not for people like him.

It began with a message.

One of the district coordinators in Sitamarhi reported a strange issue: the app had begun freezing during live sessions. Then another report came from Madhubani. Then two more from Purnia and Darbhanga. Within six hours, fifteen different field centers reported identical problems—crashes, black screens, error codes that made no sense.

Raghav rushed into the operations room where Tara already had three systems open. Zeeshan was on the phone with two field workers simultaneously, his face paler than usual.

"It's not the devices," Tara muttered. "It's the code. Something's breaking the runtime. A corrupt update, maybe."

"How many users affected?" Raghav asked.

"Too early to say. But if the update auto-pushed to all 100 blocks... it could be everyone."

Raghav's mouth dried. That was 50,000 students. 4,000 educators. Hundreds of villages that had finally started believing in the promise.

Now staring at dead screens.

By noon, screenshots flooded WhatsApp groups.

A child's tear-streaked face beside a frozen tablet.

A chalk-written note outside a rural learning center: *"Class cancelled until further notice."*

A teacher's voice note: *"We told them this would change their lives. What do we tell them now?"*

The weight in Raghav's chest turned to stone. His vision narrowed, breath sharp and mechanical. There was no time for guilt. Not now.

He pulled up the error logs, hands moving with desperation and disbelief. The update had passed internal testing. Tara had checked every script. Zeeshan had deployed it block by block.

So what had gone wrong?

Then he saw it.

A configuration file—**sync_config_v2.json**—had reverted to an older build during deployment. One line of misaligned code, a default path pointing to an outdated content schema.

It wasn't a cyberattack.

It was a human error.

His.

He had manually approved the build at 3:41 a.m., rushing through lines of code on the 38th hour of a sleepless streak.

He didn't say a word.

Just stood up and walked out.

Anika found him twenty minutes later on the stairs, sitting alone, forehead pressed to the cold metal railing.

"It was me," he said without looking at her. "I pushed the broken file. I didn't check it."

She sat beside him. "We'll fix it."

"Kids are crying, Anika. Teachers are burning. They trusted us."

"They still do. They just don't know how to say it right now."

He turned to her. "Do you?"

Anika didn't flinch. "I wouldn't be here if I didn't."

They launched **Project Repair** within the hour.

Three teams. One goal: get the system back up before the weekend.

Raghav led the backend patch.

Tara handled diagnostics and rollback staging.

Anika coordinated with the field centers to distribute instructions.

No one slept.

Zeeshan fainted from dehydration.

One of the field officers in Gaya broke down on a call and had to be calmed by Anika mid-sprint.

Meanwhile, trolls circled like vultures.

Tweets claimed the app had been "exposed." Anonymous blogs called EduInnovate a scam. A local newspaper printed a story suggesting donor fraud. Meenal Rao called with a tense voice, demanding a full incident report within twenty-four hours.

Raghav didn't respond.

He couldn't.

Not when lives—not reputations—were on the line.

Then came the second blow.

Priya's name flashed on Anika's phone. The former operations head who had walked out during the earlier fracture hadn't called since. Anika hesitated. Answered.

The voice on the other end wasn't Priya's.

It was her husband.

"Anika... it's her son. Aryan. He's in the ICU. Dengue. She asked me to inform you. She can't talk right now."

Anika's hands shook.

She walked straight to Raghav and told him everything.

He stood frozen, mouth slightly open, as if caught between rushing to Priya and holding up the burning building they'd built together.

"Go," Anika said. "She needs you more than this app does tonight."

"She won't want to see me."

"She won't say it. But she needs you."

He left without a bag. Without his laptop. Just a bottle of water and an address written on the back of a hospital flyer.

The hospital was colder than he expected. Not in temperature, but in silence. Grief hung like cobwebs in the corners.

He found Priya sitting in the corridor outside ICU-2, shoulders hunched, hands clenched around a crumpled tissue.

She looked up.

Didn't speak.

Didn't need to.

He sat beside her.

The hum of the machines was the only conversation they had for a long time.

Then, at last, she whispered, "I kept telling him not to play outside after rain. But he's six. How do you explain danger when the world is all trees and mud and joy?"

"I'm sorry," Raghav said.

"For what?" she asked. "For the app or the virus or the years between?"

"For all of it," he said.

She didn't reply.

But she didn't ask him to leave.

That was enough.

By the time Raghav returned to the office two days later, the system had stabilized.

Patch deployed.

Data restored.

App running.

But not everything had healed.

Some field workers had quit.

Some communities remained hesitant.

And yet... something had changed.

Something subtle.

In the shadows of failure and fire, a new kind of trust had emerged. Not the naive kind. Not born of promises. But forged in flame.

People had seen the team bleed. Crack. Break.

And keep going.

They weren't heroes anymore.

They were human.

And somehow, that was more powerful.

A week later, Raghav stood before a crowd of 300 village educators in Bhagalpur.

He didn't speak from a stage.

He stood on the floor, at their level, mic in hand, sweat on his brow.

He told them the truth.

About the crash. About the mistake. About the long night of rewiring.

He ended with this:

"We failed you. We will again. Because we are not perfect.
But we will always return.
We will always rebuild.
Because this is not just a platform.
It is a promise.
And I intend to keep it.
No matter the cost."

They didn't applaud.

They *stood*.

A hundred voices chanting not his name, but the name of the app.

Not as a product.

As a symbol.

As a whisper of belief.

Later that night, Anika stood beside him as he looked out at the horizon.

"What's next?" she asked.

He turned slowly.

"We build what can't break."

"How do we do that?"

He looked down at his hands.

Then back at her.

"We teach others to build it with us."

Chapter 28:
The Phoenix Pact

Ash is not just what remains after fire.

Sometimes, it is what things must become before they can be born again.

The crash had come. The failure had scorched their credibility. The apology had been made. But apologies were fragile currency. Trust—especially in villages too often betrayed—couldn't be bought back with words, or fixed with updates.

Raghav knew that.

So did Anika.

And so, as the rains tapered and the servers cooled, they sat in the middle of their war room surrounded by maps, markers, and hearts still beating despite bruises. Neither spoke for a while. Words were like glass now—useful, but capable of cutting when held too quickly.

Anika finally said what they had both been thinking.

"We can't just fix this. We need to *remake* it."

Raghav nodded slowly. "From the ashes."

She scribbled something on a yellow sticky note and stuck it to the whiteboard:

"The Phoenix Pact."

The idea was simple.

Rebuild *with* the community, not *for* it.

Give every user—not just access—but *agency*. Not just content—but *control*. Not just promises—but *power*.

The old system had been too centralized. Too dependent on the few.

This time, they would decentralize everything.

Train locals. Empower ambassadors. Distribute decision-making. Build a web, not a wall.

If a node failed, the network would survive.

If a center went dark, another would light up.

A new model.

Not a hierarchy.

A hive.

They started with eight pilot villages across Bihar and Jharkhand. Small, scattered, economically challenged but socially strong. Each was invited to elect their own **EduCatalyst**—a teacher, parent, student, or elder who would act as the local guardian of learning.

These Catalysts were trained, not just in app usage but in basic digital literacy, storytelling, curation, and feedback reporting. They were given access to the backend platform, allowing them to:

- Approve or reject content based on cultural sensitivity.

- Upload original stories, songs, riddles, and even how-to guides.
- Report technical bugs or learning difficulties directly to the core team.
- Track learning progress of their local centers and receive community impact badges.

It was no longer *EduInnovate's* app.

It was *theirs*.

At first, people laughed.

Especially outsiders.

"What, you think some farmer's wife is going to audit your database?"

"You're letting a Class 8 student approve code?"

"This isn't empowerment. It's chaos."

But Raghav had seen chaos before.

And this was not it.

This was *order*—of a different kind. An organic kind.

Messy. Unscripted. Alive.

And as the days passed, results began to bloom like monsoon lilies.

A tailor in Deoghar uploaded a visual guide on sari pleating, which got shared across 40 districts.

A retired postman from Nalanda began recording weather forecasts and agricultural tips in Magahi.

In Khagaria, a boy named Alok built his own library of science explainer videos using only a cracked Android phone and a chalkboard.

Each upload was reviewed by Catalysts, translated by volunteers, and celebrated with "Spark Stars"—virtual badges that meant little to the world but everything to the children whose voices had never been amplified.

Then something unexpected happened.

The communities didn't just engage.

They began to *compete*.

One village started holding weekly storytelling nights to generate new content.

Another created its own *mini-hackathon* where teenagers designed quizzes and puzzles for younger kids.

Women who had never touched a screen now debated content categories and app interface features.

They weren't just learning.

They were *leading*.

But not everyone was pleased.

A cluster of private edtech tutors in a Tier-3 town wrote an open letter accusing EduInnovate of disrupting their "local economy."

"Free apps," the letter read, "are making teachers obsolete."

Raghav read it twice and smiled.

Then published a public response.

"Our goal is not to replace teachers.

Our goal is to make every learner a teacher.

Education is not a job.
It is a *right to create knowledge, not just consume it.*"

The post went viral.

Again.

But this time, something had changed.

No trolls. No abuse.

Just replies like:

"My daughter just recorded her first poem in Bhojpuri. Thank you."

"We made our first story together as a family. Is there a way to add animations?"

"Do you accept uploads in Gondi too? We want to be seen."

The Phoenix Pact spread like wildfire—but a fire that warmed, not burned.

Thirty villages became sixty.

Sixty became two hundred.

New Catalysts emerged.

New voices bloomed.

Raghav watched from the sidelines, no longer the savior, but a servant to a cause that had outgrown him.

And for the first time, he welcomed it.

He didn't need to lead anymore.

He needed to *listen*.

One evening, during a community check-in, a grandmother named Shanta Devi stood up with a walking stick in one hand and a printed storybook in the other.

Her voice trembled as she spoke into the mic.

"I never went to school. I never touched a book until last year.

But last week, I read a story written by my grandson.

And for the first time, I felt like I had *entered* the world instead of watching it pass by.

You made me walk into that world.

Don't stop.
Don't turn back."

No one in the room moved for a long time.

Then, softly, Raghav clapped.

Then everyone did.

But the applause was not for him.

It was for her.

That night, Anika found Raghav sitting on the office balcony, laptop on his lap, the old silver **trishul pendant** hanging loosely around his neck.

He was uploading a new feature to the app.

"What's that?" she asked.

"Creator timeline," he said. "So every child can see how their idea grew into something that touched someone else."

She nodded. "Good. They should know they matter."

"They *do*," he said.

He turned to her, eyes shining not with exhaustion—but with reverence.

"Do you see it, Anika? This... it's no longer just a platform."

She smiled.

"I see it."

He looked up at the night sky.

No stars tonight.

But below, in villages across the plains, flickering screens glowed in the dark.

A new kind of constellation.

And they were the fire that refused to die.

Chapter 29:
Ghosts of Greatness

There is a moment in every journey where the past circles back.

Not to remind you of your roots, but to test whether you've truly left behind the ghosts that once shaped you.

For Raghav, that moment came not in a boardroom or village, but in a sleek café in Bengaluru, five floors above ground level, where cappuccinos cost more than a week's meals in Madhopur.

He had come for a roundtable on grassroots education hosted by a private philanthropic trust. But what waited for him there wasn't just discussion.

It was temptation.

Three chairs away sat Aditya Narang, co-founder of a billion-dollar EdTech unicorn. Sharp suit, white sneakers, charisma curated like a brand. His company had gamified learning into entertainment, feeding dopamine instead of discipline. Critics called it distraction. Investors called it genius.

Aditya leaned across the table mid-discussion and said, "Raghav, you're doing God's work. But why carry this burden alone? Why not exit now, cash in, and let your legacy grow without you holding the strings?"

Raghav smiled politely.

Legacy.

A beautiful word for a business obituary.

Aditya continued. "We're ready to acquire. Full absorption. We keep the name. We even keep your community model—modified, of course. You get a seat on our impact council. Advisory role. Public image. Zero stress."

And then he said the number.

Raghav didn't react. Didn't blink. But something inside him flickered.

It was enough to make the ghost stir.

That night, he sat alone in his hotel room, overlooking the blinking skyline of Bengaluru—India's so-called Silicon Valley. Neon lit the glass like fireflies trapped in a jar.

He sipped tea that tasted like regret.

And suddenly, he wasn't in the room anymore.

He was sixteen again.

Back in the internet café near Patna railway station, squinting at a cracked monitor, trying to understand how startups worked. He had idolized founders then.

Especially the ones who sold their companies and were celebrated for it.

Back then, wealth seemed like a finish line.

But now...

Now he saw their faces on magazine covers and wondered why none of them looked free.

Most of them had exited for millions—and faded into the noise. They were never remembered for what they built. Only what they sold.

Were they legends?

Or ghosts?

He called Anika.

"I got an offer."

"I figured."

She didn't sound surprised.

"What did you say?"

"I said nothing. Yet."

"Do you want it?" she asked gently.

"I don't know," he replied. "Some part of me does. The tired part."

There was silence on the line.

Then she said, "You're not tired of building, Raghav. You're tired of carrying it alone."

The line went dead before he could reply.

The next day, he flew back to Mumbai.

He found Tara waiting with a new impact report—clean graphs, steady growth. But she hesitated before handing it over.

"We found something odd," she said. "Someone tried to mirror our database schema on a third-party cloud. Internal breach attempt."

Raghav's blood chilled.

"Inside job?"

"Most likely. Zeeshan's team is investigating. Could be someone from early field days."

The ghosts, it seemed, were not just in his head.

They were in the code.

He didn't sleep that night.

Instead, he opened a document he hadn't touched in two years.

Founder's Manifesto — a digital letter he had written to himself when EduInnovate had barely 100 users. It began with a single promise:

"This will never become a product that forgets its people."

The rest of the letter was idealistic, flawed, beautiful.

He cried reading it.

Not because he felt weak.

But because he feared he was drifting.

He closed the document.

Opened a blank page.

And began writing again.

Not a pitch deck.

Not a business strategy.

A will.

Not for death.

For *survival*.

Two days later, he gathered the team in the same room where they had once nearly fallen apart. He placed two printouts on the table.

One was the acquisition offer from Aditya's company.

The other was the new **EduInnovate Constitution** — a document of values, written by community contributors, field volunteers, and learners.

He pointed at both.

And said, "We vote today. Not with hands. With our stories."

Every team member was given five minutes to speak—not about business—but about one moment where EduInnovate changed someone's life.

Anika went first. She spoke of Kanchan's comic book now taught in three districts.

Zeeshan followed with a story of a blind teacher using audio uploads to teach seven children in Arrah.

Tara shared an incident of a grandmother sending her first voice message to her daughter abroad—through the app.

By the time they were done, there was no need to vote.

Raghav picked up the acquisition letter and fed it slowly into the paper shredder.

Not out of anger.

Out of closure.

The ghost had been heard.

It no longer needed to haunt.

That evening, an email arrived from a boy in Jharkhand.

*Sir, they are asking me what I want to become.

I told them, I don't want to become anything.

I want to help others become something.

Is that allowed?*

Raghav stared at the screen, a lump forming in his throat.

He replied with a single sentence:

That's the only kind of greatness worth chasing.

And he meant every word.

Chapter 30:
The Echo Effect

The idea was planted like a seed, almost by accident.

One evening, after a storytelling session in rural Katihar, a boy named Niranjan asked a question that no one in the room expected.

"If we can write stories, can we also write books?"

The teacher chuckled. "Books are for writers, beta."

Niranjan frowned. "But aren't we writers too, if people read what we write?"

That single question rippled outward.

By morning, the ripple had become a wave.

The next week, EduInnovate's analytics dashboard lit up with a surge of unusual uploads—collections of poems, fictional tales of village monsters and talking goats, recipe instructions written by mothers, riddles passed down across generations.

These weren't just scattered submissions.

They were **books in the making**.

Each file named with ambition: *"My First Book"*, *"Tales by Grandpa"*, *"How to Make Mango Pickle in April."*

Raghav stared at the database in awe.

The users were no longer just *consuming* content.

They were *creating culture.*

It was as if a thousand whispers had gained voice and were now echoing across the plains, bouncing from screen to screen with a defiant clarity.

For years, the world had asked: "How do we teach them?"

Now, villages were asking: "Are you ready to learn from us?"

The EduInnovate app was rebuilt—again.

This time, to reflect this revolution.

The "Explore" tab now included a new section: **Village Voices.**

Every user could publish their own collection. Every story tagged by region and dialect. Readers could react not with likes, but with *seeds*—virtual acknowledgments that the story had *planted* something in them.

Soon, dozens of these "Village Books" were downloaded, translated, and narrated in local schools.

A story from Sitamarhi about a crow that refuses to fly until she learns to read was adapted into a children's play in Raipur.

A grandmother's lullaby was turned into a music video using basic animation, created by a teenager using a borrowed laptop in Nalanda.

The echoes were multiplying.

And unlike news headlines or viral tweets, these echoes *stayed*.

The change was not just cultural.

It was systemic.

In Gaya, a group of high-school girls launched their own EduInnovate-powered library, converting a former storage shed into a reading zone. Every book was user-uploaded. Every visitor earned a reading badge.

In Bokaro, former construction workers created a "Skill Bank," using the app to record and categorize hands-on tutorials in masonry, carpentry, plumbing, and tailoring.

They weren't waiting for someone to build infrastructure.

They *were* the infrastructure now.

And Raghav?

He watched it all from behind the curtain—not directing, not instructing—just observing with the quiet reverence of someone witnessing the thing he had once dreamed of... become **independent** of him.

It wasn't all smooth.

Tensions arose.

In one district, a group of private tutors demanded that community content be taken down, arguing it diluted "educational standards."

A political party tried to claim credit for the movement, even forging a logo to mimic the app.

And worst of all, a viral video circulated accusing EduInnovate of "indoctrinating" rural children with "anti-mainstream" ideas—only because a 13-year-old had published a story imagining a world without caste.

Raghav called Anika.

"Should we respond?"

She said, "The best response to noise... is echoing louder with truth."

So they did.

Not through press conferences or legal notices.

But by launching a nationwide campaign called **#OurEcho**, inviting users to share the first thing they ever learned from a story they didn't read in a book.

In seven days, 90,000 entries came in.

Folk songs.

Proverbs.

Childhood chants.

Each one a whisper from the past now pulsing into the future.

A month later, Raghav visited a school in a remote village in eastern Uttar Pradesh.

He didn't go as a founder.

He went as a listener.

There, a boy no older than eight stood in front of his class, reading from a paper he'd printed off the app.

"I wrote this story because my brother left for the city and never came back. So now he can read what I feel, even if he forgot where I live."

No one clapped.

They couldn't.

Their throats were too tight.

After class, the teacher pulled Raghav aside and said, "Do you know what you've done?"

Raghav shook his head.

"You've made them believe that what's inside them... *matters* outside."

That night, under the cover of darkness and diesel-scented air, Raghav sat on the school's tiled roof, legs dangling, eyes fixed on the vastness above.

He whispered into the void.

Not a prayer.

Not a poem.

Just one sentence.

"The echo is no longer mine. And I have never been more at peace."

When he returned to Mumbai, something in him had shifted.

He told Anika, "It's time to prepare for the day when I'm not needed."

She blinked. "Are you... leaving?"

"No," he smiled. "I'm building what I can leave behind without fear."

EduInnovate launched its final feature of the year: **Echo Labs** — self-run, self-sustained learning hubs where content came *from* the community, *for* the community, with no external moderation.

Raghav watched one of the first sessions remotely. A girl was teaching her mother how to use the app. A boy corrected his father's grammar gently. An elder clapped as her audio story played aloud for the first time.

The echo wasn't fading.

It was deepening.

Branching.

And for the first time in Raghav's life, he saw that true impact wasn't a wave that changed everything in one grand motion.

It was a whisper, repeated.

A truth, shared.

A child, seen.

And from those soft sounds...

A thunder grew.

Chapter 31:
The Whisper of Wealth

The invitation arrived not by email, but by post.

A cream-colored envelope with the government's seal pressed into the flap. Inside, a single sheet of thick, grainy paper.

You are cordially invited to receive the National Changemaker Award for Education, awarded by the Ministry of Social Development.

Venue: Madhopur Government School – your alma mater.

Date: 16th October, 10:00 AM.

Raghav stared at it for a long time.

Not because he was surprised.

But because something inside him had been waiting for this moment — not the honor, but the *return*.

Not as a prodigal son.

Not as a founder.

But as a witness to what belief, if held long enough, could become.

He arrived in Madhopur a day early, unannounced, and walked the length of the dusty roads like a ghost retracing his own legend. The banyan tree still stood tall, the old shop still sold fried pakoras in newspaper cones, and the temple bell still rang every morning at five.

But the school had changed.

Where there had once been faded blackboards and cracked windows, there were now smart screens, solar panels, and a freshly painted sign that read:

"EduInnovate Learning Hub — Powered by the People."

He stepped inside slowly, greeted by a teacher who gasped when she recognized him.

"You've come," she whispered.

He nodded. "I was always going to."

The next morning, the village gathered under a sky the color of promise — neither too blue nor too grey, just *ready*. Rows of students sat cross-legged on the courtyard floor, their uniforms crisp, their eyes wide with something deeper than admiration: *ownership.*

A small wooden stage stood at the center, decorated with marigolds, hand-drawn posters, and a banner that read:

"We Are the Writers Now."

The ceremony was short.

A few speeches. Some claps. The smell of incense mingling with fresh chalk.

When it was time, Raghav was called up.

He wore no blazer. No badge. Just a simple kurta and the silver trishul pendant that now hung around his neck like memory forged into metal.

He took the mic.

And for a moment, he didn't speak.

He looked around — at the trees, the walls, the children, the parents, the old classroom where he'd once been too afraid to raise his hand.

And then, finally, he found his voice.

"I was told once that wealth is what you earn.

I believed that.

Until I came back here and saw something different.

Wealth is not money.

It's a whisper — passed from one generation to the next.

A child teaching their mother to read.

A village teaching itself to dream.

A boy writing a story for his brother in the city.

A grandmother hearing her voice echo through a classroom.

This... *this* is wealth.

And today, I am the richest man I know."

He stepped down to silence.

Then came the first clap — small, but sharp.

Then another.

Then many.

Not applause for him.

Applause for *them*.

For all they had reclaimed.

Later that evening, long after the guests had left and the last plate of laddoos had been distributed, Raghav sat alone beneath the old neem tree behind the school.

The same one where he had once hidden from bullies. Where he had scribbled circuit diagrams in the dirt. Where he had promised himself that he would become *someone*.

He smiled.

Because now, he no longer needed to become.

He just needed to *be*.

Footsteps crunched behind him.

He turned.

It was Kanchan.

No longer the shy girl with comic dreams, but now taller, older, eyes sharper, confidence settled like armor on her shoulders.

"I have something for you," she said, and handed him a sheet.

It was a story.

Typed. Illustrated. Signed.

Title: *"The Boy Who Whispered to the Future."*

He read the first line and closed his eyes.

It wasn't about him.

It was about them all.

A generation that had turned silence into sentences.

Poverty into purpose.

Isolation into invention.

And whispers... into wealth.

As the sky darkened into starlight, Raghav leaned back against the neem tree, his body tired but his spirit still lit.

In the far distance, a girl opened the app on a secondhand phone. Her voice trembled as she read her first line aloud, her grandmother listening beside her.

And in that small sound, that uncertain but daring whisper, the story continued.

Not in chapters.

Not in reports.

But in echoes.

Endless, expanding echoes.

And in that moment, Raghav knew —

His wealth had never been counted in rupees.

It had always been counted in *belief*.

And that belief would never stop whispering.

Final Conclusion of The Book

The journey began with a single boy and a battered laptop beneath a neem tree. It ends — or begins again — with a village alight, a people awakened. EduInnovate was never just an app; it was a mirror, a bridge, a fire. In the lives touched and the courage sparked, its legacy endures. Because when forgotten voices are finally heard, they do more than echo — they transform the very world that once silenced them.

📚 Postscript: A Letter to the Future

Dear Dreamer,

If you are holding this book, I want you to know something — the world you imagine is possible. Even if you feel small. Even if your voice trembles. Even if no one claps for you right now.

You are not just building a future. You are repairing a past. One where people like you were told they couldn't, shouldn't, or wouldn't make it.

This story isn't mine anymore. It's yours. Take it, change it, expand it. Let it whisper through your struggles and shout through your victories.

Wherever you go, take your roots with you.

— The Author

💬 Reflections from the Journey

Every story begins before the first word is written. This one began in the cracks — between the places where opportunity forgot to look and talent grew anyway.

What began as a fictional tale has revealed itself to be a mirror. Of our schools. Our systems. Our silence. But also of our strength.

If even one reader finishes this book and chooses to mentor someone, believe in someone, or simply listen — then Raghav's journey was worth more than any investor pitch ever could be.

🙏 A Final Thank You

To every teacher, mentor, coder, dreamer, and stubborn believer — this story is stitched from your strength.

To the children reading this someday: You are enough. You are brilliant. Keep building.

And to you — the reader — thank you for carrying this story forward.

-The Author (Yash Vardhan Poddar)

www.ingramcontent.com/pod-product-compliance
Lightning Source LLC
LaVergne TN
LVHW041219080526
838199LV00082B/1223